# Fractions

 Keep in mind...
**If you put forth 1/2 the effort, you only get a fraction of the results.**

## Simplifying Fractions

I. Numerator Smaller than Denominator

$$\frac{4 \div 4}{8 \div 4} \text{ (greatest common factor)} = \frac{1}{2}$$

1. $\frac{6}{9}$

2. $\frac{10}{25}$

3. $\frac{7}{14}$

4. $\frac{8}{24}$

5. $\frac{36}{60}$

6. $\frac{18}{36}$

7. $\frac{8}{28}$

8. $\frac{21}{45}$

9. $\frac{12}{40}$

10. $\frac{19}{57}$

11. $\frac{20}{28}$

12. $\frac{18}{44}$

13. $\frac{36}{48}$

14. $\frac{56}{63}$

15. $\frac{5}{15}$

16. $\frac{6}{21}$

17. $\frac{40}{55}$

18. $\frac{45}{72}$

19. $\frac{12}{108}$

20. $\frac{32}{136}$

21. $\frac{24}{180}$

## ...More Simplifying

II. Numerator Larger than Denominator

$$\frac{12 \div 3}{9 \div 3} = \frac{4}{3}$$
**Improper Fraction**

$$\frac{12 \div 3}{9 \div 3} = \frac{4}{3} = \frac{3}{3} + \frac{1}{3} = 1 + \frac{1}{3} = 1\frac{1}{3}$$
**Mixed Numeral**

Write the answers as improper fractions.

1. $\frac{15}{6}$

2. $\frac{36}{27}$

3. $\frac{40}{14}$

4. $\frac{20}{12}$

5. $\frac{52}{28}$

6. $\frac{33}{27}$

7. $\frac{28}{24}$

8. $\frac{66}{27}$

9. $\frac{26}{10}$

10. $\frac{162}{48}$

11. $\frac{50}{35}$

12. $\frac{69}{18}$

13. $\frac{104}{36}$

14. $\frac{200}{56}$

15. $\frac{148}{28}$

16. $\frac{66}{9}$

Now go back and write the answers as mixed numerals.

# Adding and Subtracting Fractions

I. Like Denominators

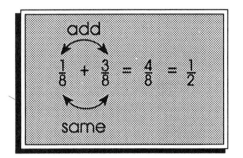

$$\text{add}$$
$$\frac{1}{8} + \frac{3}{8} = \frac{4}{8} = \frac{1}{2}$$
$$\text{same}$$

1. $\frac{2}{9} + \frac{5}{9}$

2. $\frac{3}{4} - \frac{1}{4}$

3. $\frac{9}{15} + \frac{5}{15}$

4. $\frac{19}{20} - \frac{14}{20}$

5. $\frac{27}{38} + \frac{13}{38}$

6. $\frac{35}{60} - \frac{17}{60}$

7. $\frac{17}{20} + \frac{23}{20}$

8. $\frac{25}{13} - \frac{12}{13}$

9. $\frac{11}{18} + \frac{16}{18}$

10. $\frac{17}{48} - \frac{14}{48}$

11. $\frac{7}{45} + \frac{8}{45}$

12. $\frac{33}{50} - \frac{17}{50}$

13. $\frac{16}{33} + \frac{21}{33}$

14. $\frac{43}{56} - \frac{19}{56}$

15. $\frac{12}{42} + \frac{31}{42}$

16. $\frac{29}{52} - \frac{13}{52}$

17. $\frac{15}{18} + \frac{8}{18}$

18. $\frac{43}{65} - \frac{28}{65}$

## ...More Adding and Subtracting

II. Unlike Denominators

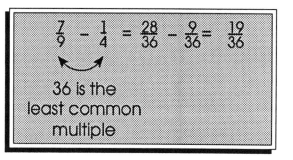

$$\frac{7}{9} - \frac{1}{4} = \frac{28}{36} - \frac{9}{36} = \frac{19}{36}$$

36 is the least common multiple

1. $\frac{2}{3} + \frac{5}{9}$

2. $\frac{4}{5} - \frac{3}{4}$

3. $\frac{5}{6} + \frac{7}{12}$

4. $\frac{11}{15} - \frac{2}{5}$

5. $\frac{11}{12} + \frac{5}{8}$

6. $\frac{1}{2} - \frac{4}{9}$

7. $\frac{13}{36} + \frac{5}{12}$

8. $\frac{7}{8} - \frac{3}{10}$

9. $\frac{5}{12} - \frac{5}{18}$

10. $\frac{5}{9} + \frac{3}{8}$

11. $\frac{5}{12} - \frac{3}{15}$

12. $\frac{3}{4} + \frac{7}{12}$

13. $\frac{8}{19} - \frac{1}{3}$

14. $\frac{7}{15} + \frac{3}{25}$

15. $\frac{30}{36} - \frac{5}{18}$

16. $\frac{4}{5} + \frac{12}{13}$

4

## ...More Adding and Subtracting (continued)

17. $\dfrac{4}{9} + \dfrac{13}{15}$

18. $\dfrac{10}{12} + \dfrac{7}{32}$

19. $\dfrac{13}{15} - \dfrac{2}{6}$

20. $\dfrac{3}{11} + \dfrac{6}{7}$

21. $\dfrac{20}{36} - \dfrac{3}{45}$

22. $\dfrac{7}{9} + \dfrac{1}{6}$

23. $\dfrac{27}{30} - \dfrac{3}{20}$

24. $\dfrac{11}{42} + \dfrac{1}{7}$

25. $\dfrac{8}{9} - \dfrac{3}{36}$

26. $\dfrac{7}{12} + \dfrac{31}{42}$

27. $\dfrac{11}{12} - \dfrac{1}{18}$

28. $\dfrac{7}{23} - \dfrac{1}{7}$

29. $\dfrac{8}{21} + \dfrac{36}{49}$

30. $\dfrac{7}{9} - \dfrac{3}{12}$

31. $\dfrac{11}{30} + \dfrac{2}{25}$

32. $\dfrac{27}{35} - \dfrac{11}{30}$

33. $\dfrac{21}{24} + \dfrac{39}{42}$

34. $\dfrac{76}{81} - \dfrac{22}{63}$

35. $\dfrac{22}{66} + \dfrac{32}{48}$

36. $\dfrac{23}{45} - \dfrac{12}{36}$

## ...And More Adding and Subtracting

III. Mixed Numerals

$$3\frac{7}{8} + 5\frac{11}{24} = 3\ \overset{\text{add}}{\frac{21}{24}} + 5\frac{11}{24} = 8\frac{32}{24} = 9\frac{8}{24} = 9\frac{1}{3}$$

1. $1\frac{1}{4} + 2\frac{1}{2}$

2. $5\frac{7}{10} - 1\frac{1}{6}$

3. $8\frac{3}{8} + 9\frac{2}{3}$

4. $6 - 2\frac{8}{11}$

5. $2\frac{1}{16} + 2\frac{1}{3}$

6. $7\frac{7}{8} - 7\frac{5}{12}$

7. $4\frac{1}{2} + 6\frac{2}{5}$

8. $5\frac{1}{2} - \frac{11}{15}$

9. $1\frac{5}{6} + 4$

10. $6\frac{7}{9} - 6\frac{1}{2}$

11. $7\frac{1}{4} + 1\frac{7}{9} + 2\frac{5}{6}$

12. $8\frac{1}{6} - 7\frac{3}{4}$

13. $5 + 3\frac{3}{11}$

14. $3\frac{5}{8} - 1\frac{6}{7}$

15. $4\frac{3}{7} + 5\frac{5}{14}$

16. $6\frac{3}{12} - 3\frac{9}{36}$

## ...And More Adding and Subtracting (continued)

17. $7 \frac{6}{15} + 2 \frac{10}{20}$

18. $10 \frac{3}{5} - 4$

19. $5 \frac{2}{9} + 7 \frac{1}{3}$

20. $11 \frac{5}{6} - 3 \frac{3}{4}$

21. $4 \frac{7}{12} + 4 \frac{3}{14}$

22. $8 - 6 \frac{5}{9}$

23. $17 \frac{14}{15} + 2 \frac{9}{10}$

24. $1 \frac{17}{18} - \frac{2}{16}$

25. $6 \frac{1}{12} + 6 \frac{3}{4}$

26. $8 \frac{2}{9} - 6 \frac{17}{18}$

27. $10 \frac{10}{16} + 3 \frac{7}{12}$

28. $2 \frac{1}{4} - 1 \frac{5}{6}$

29. $7 \frac{8}{11} + 9 \frac{1}{2}$

30. $13 - 7 \frac{1}{3}$

31. $3 \frac{5}{9} + 8 \frac{1}{6}$

32. $11 \frac{16}{22} - 4 \frac{7}{12}$

33. $7 \frac{11}{12} + 1 \frac{1}{3} + 5 \frac{3}{20}$

34. $8 \frac{1}{4} - 2 \frac{13}{14}$

35. $5 \frac{3}{15} + 12 \frac{8}{20}$

36. $9 \frac{1}{6} - 8 \frac{5}{9}$

## Multiplying Fractions

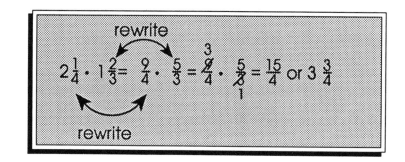

1. $\frac{1}{2} \cdot \frac{5}{6}$

2. $3 \cdot \frac{1}{2}$

3. $\frac{2}{5} \cdot \frac{1}{3}$

4. $\frac{16}{5} \cdot \frac{25}{27}$

5. $\frac{8}{21} \cdot 2\frac{7}{16}$

6. $1\frac{5}{7} \cdot 2\frac{1}{4}$

7. $5\frac{7}{8} \cdot 4$

8. $\frac{5}{7} \cdot \frac{7}{5}$

9. $3\frac{2}{3} \cdot \frac{17}{22}$

10. $\frac{5}{6} \cdot 2$

11. $8\frac{1}{3} \cdot \frac{3}{4}$

12. $4\frac{1}{4} \cdot 3\frac{1}{5}$

13. $2\frac{1}{6} \cdot \frac{18}{20}$

14. $\frac{21}{35} \cdot 3\frac{4}{7}$

15. $1\frac{3}{5} \cdot 2\frac{3}{16}$

16. $6\frac{3}{4} \cdot 1\frac{5}{9}$

17. $3\frac{1}{3} \cdot 1\frac{3}{18}$

18. $\frac{1}{2} \cdot \frac{6}{11} \cdot \frac{3}{5}$

## ...More Multiplying Fractions

1. $5\frac{3}{5} \cdot 3\frac{4}{7}$

2. $2\frac{1}{12} \cdot 2\frac{2}{15}$

3. $1\frac{1}{15} \cdot 3\frac{3}{7}$

4. $8\frac{2}{9} \cdot 2\frac{7}{8}$

5. $16 \cdot 4\frac{1}{4}$

6. $6\frac{2}{3} \cdot 1\frac{15}{16}$

7. $5\frac{3}{9} \cdot 4\frac{7}{14}$

8. $9\frac{1}{3} \cdot 8\frac{1}{10}$

9. $2\frac{1}{12} \cdot 3\frac{5}{9}$

10. $3\frac{5}{6} \cdot 8$

11. $7\frac{1}{3} \cdot \frac{9}{11}$

12. $9\frac{1}{3} \cdot 1\frac{5}{7} \cdot \frac{3}{4}$

13. $6\frac{8}{9} \cdot 3\frac{6}{7}$

14. $8\frac{2}{5} \cdot 3\frac{1}{3}$

15. $9\frac{3}{5} \cdot 2\frac{1}{12}$

16. $2\frac{1}{2} \cdot 2\frac{8}{9}$

17. $5\frac{3}{7} \cdot 2\frac{3}{16}$

18. $2\frac{1}{4} \cdot 6 \cdot 1\frac{1}{9}$

19. $4\frac{5}{10} \cdot 2\frac{2}{5}$

20. $7\frac{1}{2} \cdot 7\frac{1}{3}$

21. $3\frac{1}{8} \cdot \frac{1}{9} \cdot \frac{9}{10}$

22. $5\frac{3}{5} \cdot 4\frac{1}{2} \cdot 3\frac{1}{3}$

## Dividing Fractions

$$1\tfrac{1}{2} \div 3\tfrac{3}{7} = \tfrac{3}{2} \div \tfrac{24}{7} = \tfrac{3}{2} \cdot \tfrac{7}{24} = \tfrac{\cancel{3}}{2} \cdot \tfrac{7}{\underset{8}{\cancel{24}}} = \tfrac{7}{16}$$

invert and multiply

rewrite

1. $\dfrac{3}{7} \div \dfrac{1}{2}$

2. $\dfrac{17}{9} \div \dfrac{8}{9}$

3. $6\dfrac{2}{3} \div 5$

4. $1\dfrac{7}{9} \div 4\dfrac{2}{9}$

5. $\dfrac{15}{4} \div \dfrac{5}{14}$

6. $\dfrac{11}{12} \div \dfrac{13}{8}$

7. $4 \div 4\dfrac{2}{5}$

8. $3\dfrac{1}{4} \div 4\dfrac{3}{8}$

9. $\dfrac{6}{15} \div \dfrac{9}{10}$

10. $\dfrac{7}{8} \div 2\dfrac{1}{3}$

11. $9\dfrac{3}{8} \div 3\dfrac{3}{4}$

12. $5\dfrac{1}{6} \div \dfrac{31}{6}$

13. $\dfrac{7}{8} \div \dfrac{3}{4}$

14. $\dfrac{7}{12} \div \dfrac{7}{4}$

15. $4\dfrac{6}{7} \div \dfrac{1}{3}$

16. $5\dfrac{1}{2} \div \dfrac{7}{4}$

17. $2\dfrac{2}{9} \div 4\dfrac{2}{6}$

18. $5\dfrac{5}{12} \div 3\dfrac{1}{3}$

## ...More Dividing Fractions

1. $3\frac{3}{4} \div 2\frac{11}{12}$

2. $4\frac{4}{5} \div 2\frac{2}{15}$

3. $2\frac{1}{4} \div 5\frac{1}{4}$

4. $7\frac{5}{9} \div 8$

5. $5\frac{10}{12} \div 1\frac{2}{3}$

6. $2\frac{1}{7} \div 3\frac{4}{15}$

7. $4\frac{6}{7} \div 5\frac{8}{14}$

8. $3\frac{1}{2} \div 1\frac{9}{18}$

9. $5\frac{6}{16} \div 3\frac{9}{18}$

10. $2\frac{4}{16} \div 3\frac{2}{4}$

11. $7 \div 2\frac{5}{8}$

12. $4\frac{5}{9} \div \frac{10}{27}$

13. $6\frac{3}{7} \div 5\frac{1}{7}$

14. $2\frac{4}{9} \div 3\frac{1}{3}$

15. $6\frac{13}{20} \div 1\frac{3}{4}$

16. $5\frac{6}{9} \div 3$

17. $3\frac{3}{4} \div 2\frac{13}{26}$

18. $1\frac{7}{9} \div 4\frac{2}{9}$

19. $9\frac{3}{8} \div 3\frac{9}{12}$

20. $4\frac{3}{15} \div 1\frac{7}{20}$

21. $5\frac{3}{5} \div 3\frac{11}{15}$

22. $8\frac{1}{3} \div 3\frac{8}{9}$

## Mixed Practice with Fractions

1. $1\frac{1}{3} + \frac{5}{6}$

2. $\frac{4}{7} \cdot \frac{11}{16}$

3. $5 \div 6\frac{1}{4}$

4. $\frac{11}{17} + \frac{15}{17}$

5. $7\frac{2}{5} - 2\frac{1}{4}$

6. $2\frac{2}{3} \cdot 3\frac{3}{5}$

7. $2\frac{4}{7} \div \frac{20}{21}$

8. $\frac{42}{11} - \frac{7}{2}$

9. $\frac{5}{12} + \frac{7}{24} + \frac{31}{26}$

10. $\frac{13}{25} \cdot \frac{10}{39} \cdot \frac{15}{2}$

11. $6\frac{1}{4} - 3\frac{2}{3}$

12. $\frac{7}{2} \div \frac{5}{3}$

13. $8\frac{1}{3} + 2\frac{3}{10}$

14. $11\frac{1}{6} - \frac{5}{9}$

15. $\frac{2}{13} \cdot 3\frac{5}{7} \cdot 4\frac{1}{2}$

16. $5\frac{2}{3} \div 1\frac{2}{15}$

17. $4\frac{1}{8} + 2\frac{6}{16} - 6\frac{1}{2}$

18. $(1\frac{5}{9} \cdot 3) \div \frac{1}{3}$

19. $1\frac{4}{5} + 1\frac{1}{6} + 1\frac{1}{30}$

20. $\frac{7}{9} + (\frac{11}{12} \div \frac{33}{8})$

21. $11\frac{1}{3} - 5\frac{3}{5}$

22. $6\frac{3}{16} \cdot 3\frac{5}{9}$

## ...More Mixed Practice with Fractions

1. $8\frac{1}{15} - 5\frac{11}{20}$

2. $3\frac{1}{9} + 8\frac{3}{7} + 1\frac{1}{3}$

3. $1\frac{7}{8} \cdot 3\frac{3}{5}$

4. $4\frac{4}{5} \div 2\frac{8}{10}$

5. $3\frac{5}{12} + 5\frac{1}{4} - 2\frac{7}{20}$

6. $(\frac{16}{21} \cdot 3\frac{1}{4}) + 6\frac{1}{3}$

7. $5\frac{7}{10} - (\frac{25}{27} \div 3\frac{1}{3})$

8. $(2\frac{15}{24} + 3\frac{11}{12}) \cdot 6\frac{1}{2}$

9. $7\frac{3}{12} - 2\frac{8}{9}$

10. $1\frac{1}{6} \cdot 3\frac{5}{7} \cdot 2\frac{2}{9}$

11. $8\frac{7}{12} + 11\frac{3}{4}$

12. $7 - (3\frac{7}{9} \div 4\frac{2}{3})$

13. $2\frac{1}{2} \cdot 3\frac{3}{15}$

14. $5\frac{2}{9} - 2\frac{17}{18} + 1\frac{2}{3}$

15. $(3\frac{6}{8} \div 4\frac{2}{4}) - \frac{13}{16}$

16. $4\frac{2}{3} \cdot 1\frac{3}{4} \cdot 3\frac{3}{4}$

17. $3\frac{4}{15} + 8\frac{3}{45}$

18. $12\frac{1}{2} - 7\frac{15}{16}$

19. $(1\frac{12}{13} \cdot 7\frac{3}{5}) - 3$

20. $2\frac{1}{8} + (6\frac{2}{3} \div 8\frac{4}{9})$

21. $3\frac{1}{3} \cdot 7\frac{5}{6} \cdot 2\frac{2}{5}$

22. $1\frac{15}{16} + 3\frac{7}{24} + 3\frac{11}{12}$

## Problems with Fractions

1. If $1\frac{1}{4}$ pounds of bananas sell for 80¢ and $1\frac{1}{3}$ pounds of apples sell for 90¢, which fruit is cheaper?

2. A cake recipe calls for $\frac{2}{3}$ teaspoon salt, $1\frac{1}{2}$ teaspoons baking powder, 1 teaspoon baking soda and $\frac{1}{2}$ teaspoon cinnamon. How many total teaspoons of dry ingredients are used?

3. A baseball team played 35 games and won $\frac{4}{7}$ of them.
   How many games were won?
   How many games were lost?

4. During 4 days, the price of the stock of PEV Corporation went up $\frac{1}{4}$ of a point, down $\frac{1}{3}$ of a point, down $\frac{3}{4}$ of a point and up $\frac{7}{10}$ of a point. What was the net change?

5. Janie wants to make raisin cookies. She needs $8\frac{1}{2}$ cups of raisins for the cookies. A 15-ounce box of raisins contains $2\frac{3}{4}$ cups. How many boxes must Janie buy to make her cookies?

6. A one-half gallon carton of milk costs $1.89. A one-gallon carton of milk costs $2.99. How much money would you save if you bought a one-gallon carton instead of 2 one-half gallon cartons?

## Changing Fractions to Decimals

$$\frac{7}{20} \Rightarrow 20\overline{)\begin{array}{l}.35\phantom{0}\\7.00\\\underline{6\,0}\\1\,00\\\underline{1\,00}\\\phantom{0}0\end{array}} \Rightarrow \frac{7}{20} = .35 \quad \text{terminating}$$

$$\frac{5}{12} \Rightarrow 12\overline{)\begin{array}{l}.41666\\5.00000\\\underline{4\,8}\\20\\\underline{12}\\80\\\underline{72}\\80\\\underline{72}\\80\end{array}} \Rightarrow \frac{5}{12} = .41\overline{6} \quad \text{repeating}$$

1. $\frac{3}{5}$

2. $\frac{11}{25}$

3. $\frac{7}{15}$

4. $2\frac{1}{9}$

5. $\frac{23}{33}$

6. $1\frac{5}{16}$

7. $\frac{12}{25}$

8. $\frac{1}{3}$

9. $\frac{5}{33}$

10. $2\frac{5}{16}$

11. $\frac{25}{37}$

12. $3\frac{13}{15}$

13. $\frac{17}{22}$

14. $3\frac{11}{12}$

## ...More Changing Fractions to Decimals

1. $\frac{3}{8}$

2. $\frac{8}{15}$

3. $\frac{27}{32}$

4. $\frac{23}{30}$

5. $\frac{4}{7}$

6. $5\frac{1}{8}$

7. $1\frac{4}{5}$

8. $\frac{10}{35}$

9. $\frac{9}{15}$

10. $2\frac{7}{8}$

11. $2\frac{3}{8}$

12. $2\frac{15}{37}$

13. $\frac{67}{90}$

14. $1\frac{19}{33}$

15. $\frac{124}{333}$

16. $5\frac{7}{10}$

17. $2\frac{11}{16}$

18. $7\frac{31}{40}$

19. $3\frac{9}{16}$

20. $11\frac{24}{32}$

☞ **Keep in mind...**
**Don't wait for things to be just right**
**before you get started. Start now!**

## Rounding Decimals

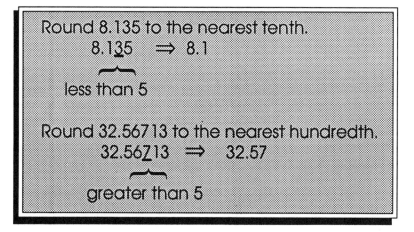

Round 8.135 to the nearest tenth.
8.1̲35 ⟹ 8.1

⏜

less than 5

Round 32.56713 to the nearest hundredth.
32.567̲13 ⟹ 32.57

⏜

greater than 5

Round to the nearest whole number.

1.  41.803      2.  119.63      3.  20.05      4.  3.45

5.  79.531      6.  8.437      7.  29.37      8.  109.96

Round to the nearest tenth.

9.  33.335      10.  1.861      11.  99.96      12.  103.103

13.  16.031      14.  281.05      15.  8.741      16.  27.773

Round to the nearest hundredth.

17.  69.713      18.  5.569      19.  609.906      20.  247.898

21.  5.535      22.  67.1951      23.  14.0305      24.  6.9372

## Multiplying and Dividing by 10, 100, etc.

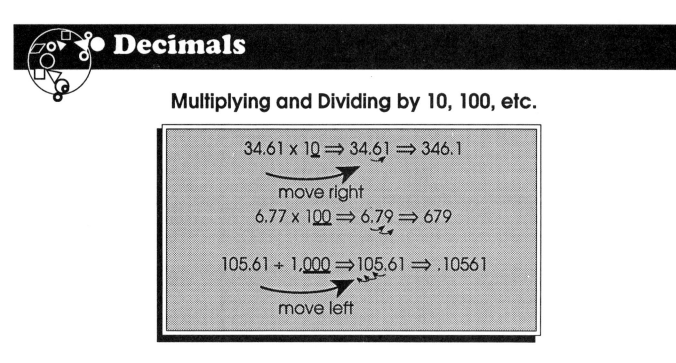

$34.61 \times 10 \Rightarrow 34.61 \Rightarrow 346.1$

move right

$6.77 \times 100 \Rightarrow 6.79 \Rightarrow 679$

$105.61 \div 1,000 \Rightarrow 105.61 \Rightarrow .10561$

move left

1.  4.81 x 100

2.  37.68 ÷ 10

3.  .46 x 1,000

4.  7.12 ÷ 10,000

5.  5.4 x 10

6.  27,500 ÷ 1,000

7.  4.395 x 100,000

8.  .0075 ÷ 100

9.  2.274 x 10

10.  90,000 ÷ 100

11.  .000618 x 1,000

12.  39.006 ÷ 1,000

13.  16 x 100

14.  28.889 ÷ 10,000

15.  36.89 x 10,000

16.  .091 ÷ 100

17.  .0336 x 100,000

18.  1,672 ÷ 100,000

## Adding Decimals

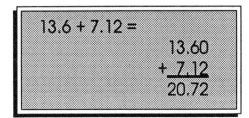

```
13.6 + 7.12 =
           13.60
         +  7.12
           20.72
```

1.  3.5 + 8.4

2.  43.57 + 104.6

3.  15.36 + 29.23 + 7.2

4.  7.6 + 12.412

5.  2.304 + 6.18 + 9.2

6.  $12.91 + $6.99

7.  .08 + 19

8.  16.234 + .0019

9.  22.16 + .193 + 72

10.  110.6 + .983

11.  18.662 + 2.54

12.  1.398 + 106

13.  $17.72 + $23.60

14.  22.63 + 1,694

15.  322.814 + 5.667

16.  362.1 + 8.888 + .016

17.  1,392.16 + 16.16

18.  83.196 + .0017

## Subtracting Decimals

$$12 - 3.78 =$$
$$\begin{array}{r} 12.00 \\ -\ 3.78 \\ \hline 8.22 \end{array}$$

1. 17.6 – 9.3

2. 21.3 – 16.5

3. 32.3 – 12.72

4. 83.06 – 12.3

5. 291.36 – 187.837

6. 23.96 – 19.931

7. $29.98 – $16.09

8. 6.192 – .08

9. 63.36 – .007 – 1.1

10. 16.22 – .039

11. 44.44 – 16.103

12. 102.8 – 16.61 – .099

13. 1,892 – .892

14. $75.02 – $3.99

15. 732.32 – 55.5

16. 575.021 – 65.98

17. 663.09 – 12.1227

18. 394.6 – 27.88 – .0933

## Multiplying Decimals

$$(.7)\,(.04) \quad = \quad \begin{array}{r} .7 \\ \underline{\times .04} \\ .028 \end{array}$$

$(.7)\,(.04)$ → 3 decimal places

.028 → 3 decimal places

1. (.003) (6)

2. (.051) (.003)

3. (260) (.01)

4. (9.6) (5)

5. (7) (3.42)

6. (5.29) (11.3)

7. (.017) (6.2)

8. (.3) (.03) (.003)

9. (1.5) (.096) (4.3)

10. (.05) (.16) (.001)

11. (8) (.217) (.01)

12. (18) (.08)

13. (16.01) (.5) (.31)

14. (1.06) (.005)

15. (4.802) (11.11)

16. (10.25) (.331)

17. (5) (1.102)

18. (12.8) (.05) (3.09)

## ...More Multiplying Decimals

1. (20) (.011)

2. (12.8) (.12)

3. (1.8) (6.03)

4. (34.1) (1.4)

5. (7.21) (22.2)

6. (55) (.033)

7. (6.9) (11)

8. (6.7) (.801)

9. (8.2) (.1) (.002)

10. (.005) (.011)

11. (4.04) (4.04)

12. (32.1) (2.02)

13. (5.7) (.2) (.07)

14. (.6) (17) (.05)

15. (.13) (8.5) (.5)

16. (9.8) (2.8) (1.8)

17. (21.21) (.9) (.01)

18. (10.6) (4.3) (.8)

19. (66.2) (11)

20. (.84) (.07) (.08)

## Dividing Decimals

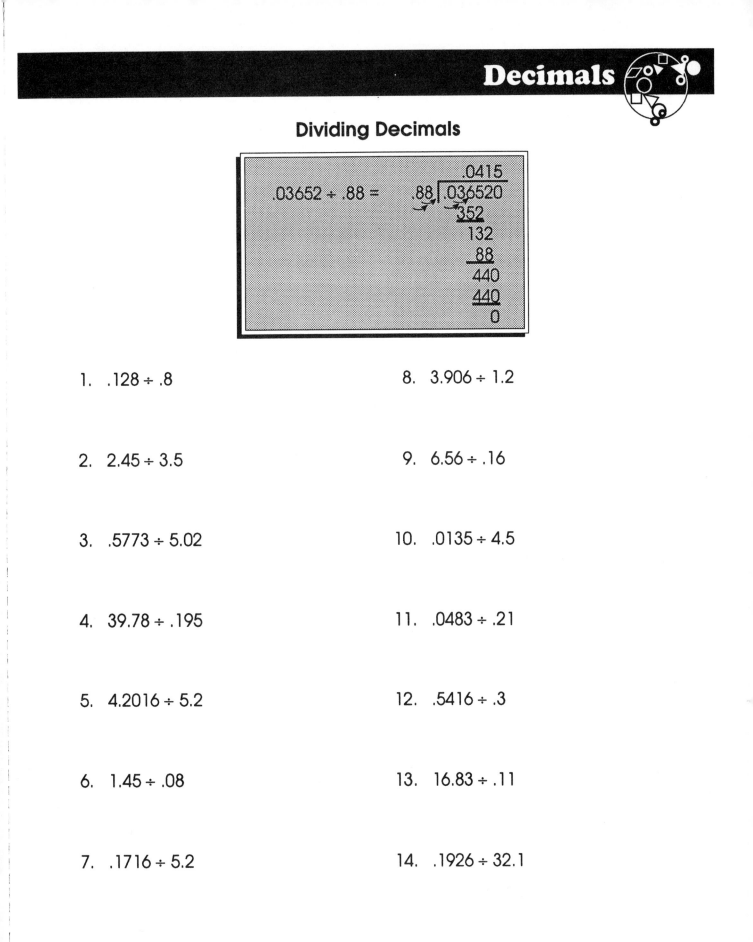

$$.03652 \div .88 = \quad .88\overline{\smash){.036520}}$$

$$\begin{array}{r} .0415 \\ .88\overline{)\,.036520} \\ \underline{352} \\ 132 \\ \underline{88} \\ 440 \\ \underline{440} \\ 0 \end{array}$$

1. $.128 \div .8$

2. $2.45 \div 3.5$

3. $.5773 \div 5.02$

4. $39.78 \div .195$

5. $4.2016 \div 5.2$

6. $1.45 \div .08$

7. $.1716 \div 5.2$

8. $3.906 \div 1.2$

9. $6.56 \div .16$

10. $.0135 \div 4.5$

11. $.0483 \div .21$

12. $.5416 \div .3$

13. $16.83 \div .11$

14. $.1926 \div 32.1$

23

## ...More Dividing Decimals

1. $72.14 \div 5$

2. $8.32 \div .8$

3. $6.29 \div .02$

4. $21.76 \div 3.2$

5. $.458 \div .06$

6. $6.15 \div .82$

7. $428.4 \div 51$

8. $24 \div .8$

9. $18.6 \div 8$

10. $.816 \div .16$

11. $20.3 \div 4$

12. $3.64 \div 1.3$

13. $.315 \div .05$

14. $38.916 \div .92$

15. $.0585 \div 4.5$

16. $295.03 \div 16.3$

17. $1.4553 \div 3.3$

18. $2.8616 \div 2.8$

19. $119.889 \div 17.3$

20. $809.34 \div 32.9$

## Mixed Practice with Decimals

1. $12.16 - 8.72$

2. $119.7 + 11.97$

3. $(3.4) (8)$

4. $2960 \div .37$

5. $1.21 \div 1.1$

6. $7 + 6.91$

7. $18.91 - 11.857$

8. $(1.35) (21.4)$

9. $21.2 - 9.03$

10. $.7 + .02 + 4$

11. $(.25) (2.5) (25)$

12. $95.6 - 87.81 + 12.21$

13. $(.8) (1.3) (.62)$

14. $37.92 \div 1.2$

15. $.1007 \div 5.3$

16. $329.82 + 6.129$

17. $893.631 - 11.09$

18. $18.332 + 82.82$

19. $132.03 \div 8.1$

20. $(16.1) (3.66)$

21. $1093.62 - 10.993$

22. $6.963 \div 2.11$

## ...More Mixed Practice with Decimals

1.  18.32 + 1.363

2.  16.3 − 5.56

3.  (3.1) (8.6)

4.  49.28 ÷ 5.6

5.  (19.2) (2.3)

6.  26.89 + 323.9

7.  19.83 − 1.326

8.  92.4 ÷ 5.5

9.  303.12 + 62.63

10. (23.1) (.13)

11. 629.2 − 11.113

12. 301.09 − 18.62

13. 24.64 ÷ 7.7

14. 1.993 + 20.93

15. (5.65) (3.9)

16. 5.052 ÷ .12

17. 333.3 − 62.91

18. 1032.8 + 10.101

19. 25.276 ÷ .71

20. (10.8) (6.12)

21. 609.82 + 11.1 − 96.812

22. (.492 ÷ .6) + 13.3

## Problems with Decimals

1. Jim's gas credit card bill was $80.97 for June, $41.35 for July and $65.08 for August. What were his total charges for the summer?

2. One cup of hot chocolate can be made with .18 ounces of hot chocolate mix. How many cups can be made from a 6.48 ounce canister of mix?

3. Karl's car payments are $215.37 per month for the next three years. What will be the total amount he will pay for his car?

4. The dress Sally wants costs $85.15. If the price was reduced by $12.78, how much will she pay?

5. Melissa went to the mall and noticed that the price of a coat she wanted was cut in half! The original price was $58.22. What is the sales price?

6. Tyler decided that he wanted a dog. He went to the pet store and bought one for $42.95. Tyler also bought three bags of food for $12.55 a bag. How much did Tyler spend altogether?

7. Christopher decided to make his grandmother a birdhouse instead of buying her one. The materials for the birdhouse totaled $21.99. The cost of a new birdhouse is $37.23. How much did Christopher save?

8. Jim thinks that snow skiing looks like lots of fun. He decided he wants to try it. First he needs equipment. He bought a pair of skis for $129.78, a pair of boots for $62.22, poles for $12.95, a hat for $2.50, a coat for $49.95, ski pants for $27.50 and gloves for $11.25. How much did Jim spend altogether?

## Changing Decimals to Fractions

Terminating Decimals

$$.25 = \frac{25}{100} = \frac{1}{4}$$

$$.132 = \frac{132}{1000} = \frac{33}{250}$$

Repeating Decimals

$$N = .\overline{12} = .121212...$$

$$100N = 12.1212...$$

$$- \quad N = - \ .1212...$$

$$\frac{99N}{99} = \frac{12}{99}$$

$$N = \frac{4}{33}$$

or $.\overline{12} = \frac{4}{33}$

1. $.125$

2. $.\overline{6}$

3. $.36$

4. $.\overline{46}$

5. $.6875$

6. $.91\overline{6}$

7. $.625$

8. $.\overline{27}$

9. $.3\overline{8}$

10. $.55$

11. $.5625$

12. $.775$

# Ratios, Proportions and Percents

 **Keep in mind...**
**Life is 10% what you make it**
**amd 90% how you take it.**

## Ratios

Write each ratio as a fraction in simplest form.

$$3 \text{ to } 12 \Rightarrow \frac{3}{12} = \frac{1}{4} \qquad 65 : 35 \Rightarrow \frac{65}{35} = \frac{13}{7}$$

$$6 \text{ out of } 40 \Rightarrow \frac{6}{40} = \frac{3}{20}$$

1. 196 to 7

2. 19 : 76

3. 18 out of 27

4. $\frac{3}{8}$ to $\frac{3}{4}$

5. .11 : 1.21

6. 140 : 112

7. 18 to 27

8. 54 out of 87

9. 112 : 140

10. 88 to 104

11. 65 out of 105

12. 65 : 117

13. 165 to 200

14. 168 : 264

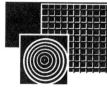

## Proportions

Solve each proportion.

$$\frac{3}{7} = \frac{x}{49}$$

$$3 \cdot 49 = 7x$$

$$\frac{147}{7} = \frac{7x}{7}$$

$$21 = x$$

1. $\dfrac{8}{6} = \dfrac{m}{27}$

2. $\dfrac{z}{3} = \dfrac{8}{15}$

3. $\dfrac{16}{40} = \dfrac{24}{c}$

4. $\dfrac{9}{p} = \dfrac{5}{2}$

5. $\dfrac{1.8}{x} = \dfrac{3.6}{2.4}$

6. $\dfrac{4}{5} = \dfrac{.8}{y}$

7. $\dfrac{x}{2} = \dfrac{15}{5}$

8. $\dfrac{18}{12} = \dfrac{24}{x}$

9. $\dfrac{18}{15} = \dfrac{6}{x}$

10. $\dfrac{121}{x} = \dfrac{220}{100}$

11. $\dfrac{1.6}{x} = \dfrac{14}{21}$

12. $\dfrac{x}{168} = \dfrac{66^2/_3}{100}$

13. $\dfrac{x}{32} = \dfrac{37^1/_2}{100}$

14. $\dfrac{16}{48} = \dfrac{x}{100}$

15. $\dfrac{.12}{.25} = \dfrac{x}{100}$

16. $\dfrac{1.5}{x} = \dfrac{.07}{.14}$

## Problems Using Proportions

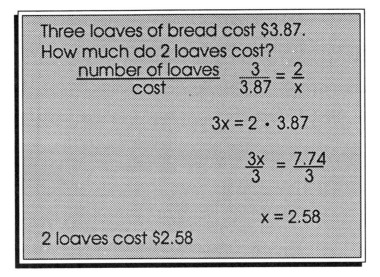

Three loaves of bread cost $3.87.
How much do 2 loaves cost?

$$\frac{\text{number of loaves}}{\text{cost}} \quad \frac{3}{3.87} = \frac{2}{x}$$

$$3x = 2 \cdot 3.87$$

$$\frac{3x}{3} = \frac{7.74}{3}$$

$$x = 2.58$$

2 loaves cost $2.58

1. If 64 feet of rope weigh 20 pounds, how much will 80 feet of the same type of rope weigh?

2. If a 10 pound turkey takes 4 hours to cook, how long will it take a 14 pound turkey to cook?

3. An 18 ounce box of cereal costs $2.76. How many ounces should a box priced at $2.07 contain?

4. Mike and Pat traveled 392 miles in 7 hours. If they travel at the same rate, how long will it take them to travel 728 miles?

5. If 2 pounds of turkey costs $1.98, what should 3 pounds cost?

6. If 2 liters of fruit juice cost $3.98, how much do 5 liters cost?

7. A 12 ounce box of cereal costs $.84. How many ounces should be in a box marked $.49?

8. Janie saw an advertisement for a 6 ounce tube of toothpaste that costs $.90. How much should a 4 ounce tube cost?

## Percents

Write each expression as a percent.

$$\frac{3}{4} \Rightarrow \frac{3}{4} = \frac{x}{100}$$
$$300 = 4x$$
$$75 = x$$
$$\frac{3}{4} = 75\%$$

$$.375 \Rightarrow .375 = 37.5\%$$

Move decimal 2 places
to the right.

1. $\frac{4}{5}$

2. $\frac{4}{7}$

3. .22

4. 2.5

5. $\frac{3}{8}$

6. .006

7. 1.125

8. $\frac{1}{2}$

9. $\frac{9}{40}$

10. 11.3

11. $\frac{11}{20}$

12. .086

13. $\frac{7}{8}$

14. 16.688

15. $\frac{7}{16}$

16. 621.9

17. $\frac{5}{16}$

18. 3.9932

32

## ...More Percents

Write each percent as a fraction.

$$90\% \qquad 61.5\%$$
$$90\% = \frac{90}{100} = \frac{9}{10} \qquad 61.5\% = \frac{61.5}{100} = \frac{615}{1000} = \frac{123}{200}$$

1.  50%

2.  45%

3.  $33\frac{1}{3}\%$

4.  7.4%

5.  31%

6.  125%

7.  $16\frac{2}{3}\%$

8.  62.5%

9.  $21\frac{1}{4}\%$

10. 32.4%

11. $8\frac{3}{4}\%$

12. 6.25%

13. $16\frac{1}{5}\%$

14. 1,189%

15. $32\frac{1}{8}\%$

16. $21\frac{4}{5}\%$

17. 18.16%

18. $101\frac{1}{2}\%$

# Ratios, Proportions and Percents

## Working with Percents

I.

| $80\% \text{ of } 30 = \underline{\hspace{1cm}}$ |
| --- |
| $\dfrac{80}{100} = \dfrac{x}{30}$ |
| $100x = 2400$ |
| $x = 24$ |

1. $20\% \text{ of } 10 = \underline{\hspace{1cm}}$   4. $9\frac{1}{2}\% \text{ of } 20 = \underline{\hspace{1cm}}$

2. $25\% \text{ of } 45 = \underline{\hspace{1cm}}$   5. $25\% \text{ of } 39 = \underline{\hspace{1cm}}$

3. $88\% \text{ of } 15 = \underline{\hspace{1cm}}$   6. $16\% \text{ of } 90 = \underline{\hspace{1cm}}$

II.

| $\underline{\hspace{1cm}}\% \text{ of } 40 = 10$ |
| --- |
| $\dfrac{x}{100} = \dfrac{10}{40}$ |
| $40x = 1000$ |
| $x = 25 \quad 25\%$ |

1. $\underline{\hspace{1cm}}\% \text{ of } 25 = 15$   4. $\underline{\hspace{1cm}}\% \text{ of } 75 = 33$

2. $\underline{\hspace{1cm}}\% \text{ of } 30 = 10$   5. $\underline{\hspace{1cm}}\% \text{ of } 15 = 6$

3. $\underline{\hspace{1cm}}\% \text{ of } 4 = 7$   6. $\underline{\hspace{1cm}}\% \text{ of } 80 = 40$

II.

| $50\% \text{ of } \underline{\hspace{1cm}} = 65$ |
| --- |
| $\dfrac{50}{100} = \dfrac{65}{x}$ |
| $50x = 6500$ |
| $x = 130$ |

1. $20\% \text{ of } \underline{\hspace{1cm}} = 15$   4. $33\frac{1}{3}\% \text{ of } \underline{\hspace{1cm}} = 41$

2. $80\% \text{ of } \underline{\hspace{1cm}} = 56$   5. $80\% \text{ of } \underline{\hspace{1cm}} = 16$

3. $25\% \text{ of } \underline{\hspace{1cm}} = 19$   6. $30\% \text{ of } \underline{\hspace{1cm}} = 15$

# Ratios, Proportions and Percents

## Problems with Percents

1. In a group of 60 children, 12 have brown eyes. What percent have brown eyes?

2. A salesman makes a 5% commission on all he sells. How much does he have to sell to make $1500?

3. A sales tax of $5\frac{3}{4}$% is charged on a blouse priced at $42. How much sales tax must be paid?

4. A baby weighed 7.6 pounds at birth and $9\frac{1}{2}$ pounds after 6 weeks. What was the percent increase?

5. A scale model of a building is 8% of actual size. If the model is 1.2 meters tall, how tall is the building?

6. The purchase price of a camera is $84. The carrying case is 12% of the purchase price. Find the total cost including the carrying case.

7. The regular price of a record cost is $15. Find the discount and the new price if there is a 20% discount.

8. A basketball team played 45 games. They won 60% of them. How many did the team win?

9. A test had 50 questions. Joe got 70% of them correct. How many did Joe get correct?

10. Diet soda contains 90% less calories than regular soda. If a can of regular soda contains 112 calories, how many calories does a can of diet soda contain?

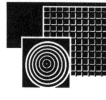

## Can You De-Code This Puzzle?

Decipher the code and perform the indicated operations.

|  |  |  |
|---|---|---|
| .3 | $\frac{1}{20}$ | 2.1 |
| $3\frac{1}{10}$ | 2.8 | $\frac{8}{25}$ |
| 4 | .1 | $\frac{1}{2}$ |

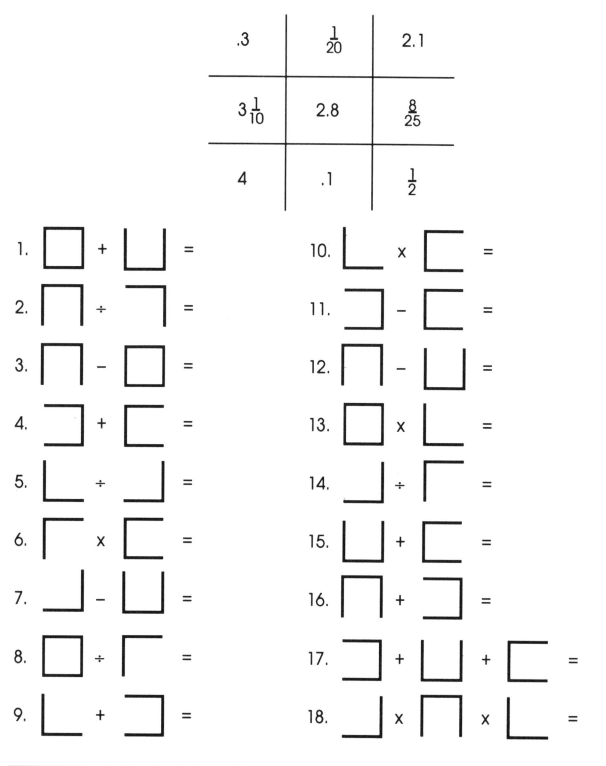

1. ☐ + ☐ =

2. ☐ ÷ ☐ =

3. ☐ – ☐ =

4. ☐ + ☐ =

5. ☐ ÷ ☐ =

6. ☐ x ☐ =

7. ☐ – ☐ =

8. ☐ ÷ ☐ =

9. ☐ + ☐ =

10. ☐ x ☐ =

11. ☐ – ☐ =

12. ☐ – ☐ =

13. ☐ x ☐ =

14. ☐ ÷ ☐ =

15. ☐ + ☐ =

16. ☐ + ☐ =

17. ☐ + ☐ + ☐ =

18. ☐ x ☐ x ☐ =

# Integers

☞ Keep in mind...
To succeed—Do the best you can,
where you are, with what you have.

## Positive and Negative Numbers

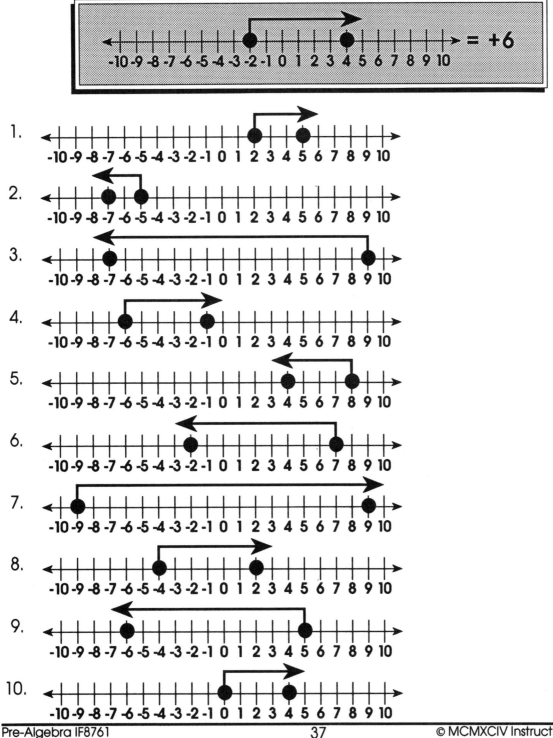

37

## Adding Integers (Number Line)

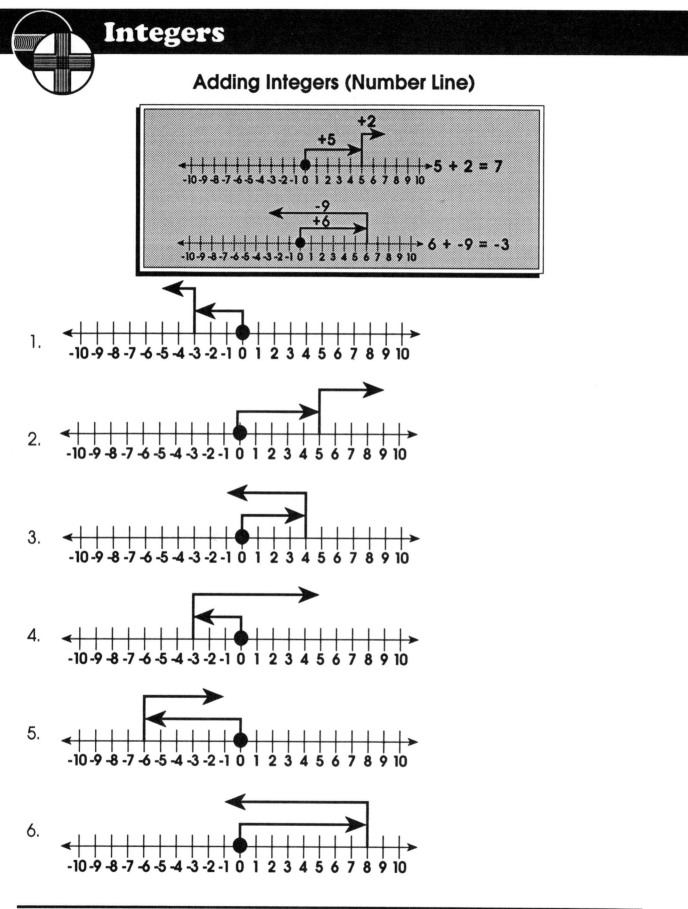

1.

2.

3.

4.

5.

6.

## Adding Integers with Like Signs

| 5 + 5 | = | 10 |
|---|---|---|
| 2 positives | | positive |
| -3 + -12 | = | -15 |
| 2 negatives | | negative |

1. 6 + 8

2. -9 + -23

3. 25 + 37

4. -85 + -19

5. 132 + 899

6. -104 + -597

7. -642 + -33

8. 88 + 298

9. -45 + -68

10. -12 + -18 + -35

11. 21 + 108 + 111

12. -62 + -33 + -12

13. 17 + 39 + 44

14. -18 + -18 + -18

15. 19 + 42 + 647

16. -29 + -108 + -337 + -503

## ...More Adding Integers with Like Signs

1. $16 + 26$

2. $-8 + -36$

3. $28 + 31$

4. $-121 + -93$

5. $-622 + -881$

6. $282 + 83$

7. $-537 + -691$

8. $-96 + -36$

9. $6,811 + 833$

10. $1,832 + 16,631$

11. $-8,693 + -11,192$

12. $15,931 + 4,489$

13. $-11,121 + -16,899$

14. $37,454 + 88,697$

15. $-101,997 + -45,532$

16. $-677,762 + -89,999$

17. $525 + 63 + 8,121$

18. $-18,619 + -45,697 + -21,112$

19. $-18,161 + -11,132 + -6,866$

20. $682,914 + 683,319 + 51,132$

21. $22,633 + 984,116 + 55,256$

22. $-119,194 + -83,677 + -43,288$

23. $-212,201 + -48,809 + -56,009$

24. $66,683 + 102,259 + 83,387$

## Adding Integers with Unlike Signs

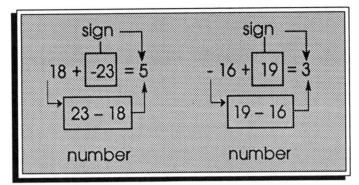

1. 2 + -8

2. -19 + 8

3. 25 + -5

4. -16 + 32

5. -319 + 319

6. -285 + 116

7. 46 + -29

8. -8 + 8

9. 852 + -468

10. -98 + 104

11. -63 + 41

12. 418 + -586

13. -1,126 + 866

14. 16,892 + -32,899

15. 43,111 + -16,832

16. -525,109 + 85,989

## ...More Adding Integers with Unlike Signs

1.  21 + -87

2.  -63 + 59

3.  12 + -12

4.  -28 + 82

5.  -32 + 97

6.  -53 + 74

7.  132 + –87

8.  212 + -99

9.  -331 + 155

10. -413 + 521

11. 8,129 + -6,312

12. -11,332 + 566

13. 1,627 + -7,193

14. 7,864 + -6,329

15. -10,822 + 6,635

16. 13,894 + -81,139

17. -16,742 + 65,524

18. -56,814 + 73,322

19. 101,811 + -322,885

20. 562,493 + -112,819

21. 116,667 + -912,182

22. -629,922 + 81,962

23. -196,322 + 422, 899

24. 467,833 + -36,838

## Subtracting Integers

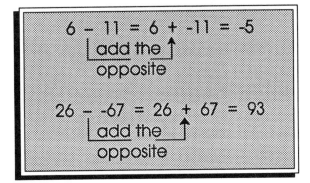

1.  19 – 23

2.  -8 – 7

3.  35 – 20

4.  -46 – -18

5.  -118 – 12

6.  7 – -103

7.  211 – 108

8.  -9 – -16

9.  63 – 72

10. -93 – 117

11. 45 – -50

12. -18 – -12

13. 21 – 82

14. -831 – 616

15. -632 – -714

16. 1,192 – -983

---

## ...More Subtracting Integers

1. 7 – 13

2. -17 – 9

3. -11 – 7

4. -24 – -23

5. 2 – 25

6. 0 – -14

7. -3 – -7

8. -8 – -27

9. -29 – 36

10. -72 – -84

11. 63 – 94

12. 77 – -27

13. -72 – -84

14. -70 – 18

15. 318 – -864

16. -626 – 118

17. 553 – -764

18. -832 – 1,129

19. 6,793 – -8,329

20. -7,624 – 11,652

21. 108,719 – -96,989

22. -832,629 – -163,864

23. -629,299 – 532,106

24. 735,300 – -800,919

## Adding & Subtracting Integers

1.  -6 + -8

2.  -10 – 3

3.  -14 + 20

4.  31 – -9

5.  -17 + 9

6.  -8 – -27

7.  -33 – 36

8.  19 + -32

9.  112 – -52

10. 0 – -7

11. 24 + -24

12. 508 – 678

13. -23 – -28

14. 0 – 31

15. -40 – 35

16. 73 + -19

17. -231 – -231

18. -107 + -293

19. 52 + -41 – 60

20. -85 – -106 + 18

21. 81 – 165 – -75

22. -16 + 312 + -621

23. -121 + -632 – -11

24. -553 – -632 + -85

## Multiplying Integers

$(4)\,(4) = 16$     $(-8)\,(-6) = 48$     $(-5)\,(10) = -50$
$+ \cdot + = +$       $- \cdot - = +$         $- \cdot + = -$

Like Signs $\Rightarrow$ Positive      Unlike Signs $\Rightarrow$ Negative

1. $(-3)\,(-6)$

2. $(14)\,(-4)$

3. $(25)\,(2)$

4. $(20)\,(-49)$

5. $(75)\,(15)$

6. $(-30)\,(-30)$

7. $(-17)\,(23)$

8. $(-218)\,(-32)$

9. $(801)\,(-37)$

10. $(-89)\,(-321)$

11. $(31)\,(-31)\,(31)$

12. $(-4)\,(-18)\,(28)$

13. $(-53)\,(-14)\,(-7)$

14. $(32)\,(125)\,(11)$

15. $(-37)\,(-18)\,(-5)\,(2)$

16. $(111)\,(-63)\,(19)$

17. $(20)\,(-7)\,(35)\,(-3)$

18. $(16)\,(-8)\,(-10)\,(-1)$

19. $(-9)\,(-29)\,(32)\,(2)$

20. $(-18)\,(-6)\,(-21)\,(-30)$

## ...More Multiplying Integers

1. (6) (6)

2. (-8) (9)

3. (-8) (2)

4. (-11) (-7)

5. (-4) (3) (-2)

6. (6) (-5) (-5) (-1)

7. (23) (-12)

8. (-15) (-15)

9. (31) (22)

10. (43) (-39)

11. (-101) (33)

12. (-56) (-207)

13. (-16) (126)

14. (-56) (-82)

15. (-86) (-212)

16. (116) (-120)

17. (-20) (-36) (-42)

18. (91) (-16) (45)

19. (-63) (18) (-21)

20. (212) (7) (33)

21. (125) (-18) (-73) (-2)

22. (-108) (-16) (-201) (-3)

23. (-52) (8) (-103) (21)

24. (16) (72) (-18) (-6)

## Dividing Integers

$$\frac{-24}{-8} = 3 \qquad\qquad -32 \div 4 = -8$$

$$\frac{\div}{\div} = + \qquad\qquad - \div + = -$$

Like Signs $\Rightarrow$ Positive     Unlike Signs $\Rightarrow$ Negative

1. $-49 \div 7$

2. $100 \div -4$

3. $-75 \div -15$

4. $-84 \div 21$

5. $-120 \div 5$

6. $57 \div -19$

7. $-288 \div -4$

8. $804 \div 67$

9. $\dfrac{17}{-17}$

10. $\dfrac{-72}{-18}$

11. $\dfrac{-195}{13}$

12. $\dfrac{-23}{-1}$

13. $\dfrac{200}{10}$

14. $\dfrac{270}{-45}$

15. $\dfrac{-343}{7}$

16. $\dfrac{-1125}{-45}$

48

## ...More Dividing Integers

1.  -81 ÷ -9

2.  13 ÷ -13

3.  -60 ÷ 10

4.  -88 ÷ -11

5.  144 ÷ 12

6.  -104 ÷ 8

7.  -147 ÷ -21

8.  80 ÷ -5

9.  72 ÷ 4

10.  -150 ÷ -6

11.  $\dfrac{-102}{17}$

12.  $\dfrac{-75}{-5}$

13.  $\dfrac{196}{-14}$

14.  $\dfrac{-468}{-26}$

15.  $\dfrac{253}{11}$

16.  $\dfrac{-256}{16}$

17.  $\dfrac{-465}{-31}$

18.  $\dfrac{-552}{-23}$

19.  $\dfrac{1378}{-26}$

20.  $\dfrac{-1824}{-48}$

## Mixed Practice with Integers

1. $-41 + -125$

2. $79 - 88$

3. $-3 \cdot -4$

4. $\dfrac{-125}{5}$

5. $19 \cdot -24$

6. $\dfrac{-123}{41}$

7. $82 + -95$

8. $27 - -46$

9. $-31 - -32$

10. $\dfrac{-825}{-33}$

11. $-34 + 52 + -18$

12. $14 \cdot -12 \cdot 3$

13. $\dfrac{-185}{5} \cdot -4$

14. $76 - 19 + -60$

15. $17 - -12 - 22$

16. $100 \cdot -4 \cdot 40$

17. $\dfrac{54}{-9} + \dfrac{33}{11} + \dfrac{24}{8}$

18. $-51 \div 17$

19. $4 - 8 + -9$

20. $\dfrac{-98}{49} \cdot -10$

21. $(256 \div -16) \cdot -3$

22. $(-18 - -26 + -13) \cdot -2$

23. $(202 + -196 - 321) \div -5$

24. $(\dfrac{-575}{23} - 18) \cdot -11$

## Problems with Integers

1. An elevator started at the first floor and went up 18 floors. It then came down 11 floors and went back up 16. At what floor was it stopped?

2. At midnight, the temperature was 30° F. By 6:00 a.m., it had dropped 5° and by noon, it had increased by 11°. What was the temperature at noon?

3. Some number added to 5 is equal to -11. Find the number.

4. From the top of a mountain to the floor of the valley below is 4,392 feet. If the valley is 93 feet below sea level, what is the height of the mountain?

5. During one week, the stock market did the following: Monday rose 18 points, Tuesday rose 31 points, Wednesday dropped 5 points, Thursday rose 27 points and Friday dropped 38 points. If it started out at 1,196 on Monday, what did it end up on Friday?

6. An airplane started at 0 feet. It rose 21,000 feet at takeoff. It then descended 4,329 feet because of clouds. An oncoming plane was approaching, so it rose 6,333 feet. After the oncoming plane passed, it descended 8,453 feet. At what feet was the plane flying?

7. Some number added to -11 is 37. Divide this number by -12. Then, multiply by -8. What is the final number?

8. Jim decided to go for a drive in his car. He started out at 0 miles per hour (mph). He then accelerated 20 mph down his street. Then, to get on the highway he accelerated another 35 miles per hour. A car was going slow in front of him so he slowed down 11 mph. He then got off the highway, so he slowed down another 7 mph. At what speed is he driving?

☞ | Keep in mind...
Luck may sometimes help but work always does.

## Adding and Subtracting Rational Numbers

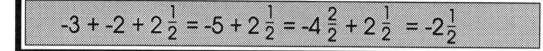

$$-3 + -2 + 2\frac{1}{2} = -5 + 2\frac{1}{2} = -4\frac{2}{2} + 2\frac{1}{2} = -2\frac{1}{2}$$

1.  $-1.6 + 1\frac{7}{10}$

    (Hint: $1\frac{7}{10} = 1.7$)

2.  $0 - 6\frac{1}{2} + -3$

3.  $-\frac{3}{4} + 5 - \frac{1}{2}$

4.  $9 - 10.2 + -8.6$

5.  $\frac{1}{2} + 1\frac{1}{2} - 1\frac{1}{3}$

6.  $6.75 - 3\frac{1}{2} + 2.55$

    (Hint: $3\frac{5}{10} = 3.5$)

7.  $3\frac{3}{7} - -1\frac{1}{7} + \frac{3}{7}$

8.  $-7 - -2\frac{3}{4} + -5\frac{1}{4}$

9.  $7\frac{1}{10} + -7.25 - 11.39$

10.  $-8\frac{1}{4} + -3\frac{3}{12} - 7\frac{2}{3}$

11.  $-5 - 7\frac{1}{8} + -3\frac{5}{12}$

12.  $3\frac{3}{10} + -3.38 - 6\frac{6}{10}$

## ...More Adding and Subtracting Rational Numbers

1. $-3\frac{5}{10} + 8$

2. $-5\frac{3}{7} + -3\frac{3}{14}$

3. $6\frac{1}{6} - 6\frac{3}{10}$

4. $-8 + 15.32$

5. $-8\frac{3}{10} - -5.9$

6. $13 - 5\frac{3}{5}$

7. $12\frac{1}{9} + -5\frac{2}{3}$

8. $-11.03 - -21.6$

9. $-7\frac{3}{10} - 16.53$

10. $31\frac{8}{9} + -27\frac{27}{81}$

11. $11 - 18.6 + -3\frac{3}{10}$

12. $-5\frac{2}{10} + 16.7 - 3\frac{1}{5}$

13. $13\frac{1}{3} + -12 + -7\frac{7}{12}$

14. $41.32 + -18.7 - 16.21$

15. $-18.75 - 5\frac{3}{4} - 7\frac{5}{12}$

16. $-15 - 21\frac{1}{7} + 18\frac{2}{49}$

17. $7\frac{2}{3} + -8\frac{4}{9} - -16\frac{1}{6}$

18. $-31.5 - -3\frac{7}{10} + 21$

19. $25\frac{1}{5} - 17.3 + -11\frac{2}{11}$

20. $19.25 - -6\frac{3}{4} + 12\frac{5}{12}$

# Rational Numbers

## Multiplying and Dividing Rational Numbers

$$-4 \cdot 5 \cdot \frac{1}{2} = -20 \cdot \frac{1}{2} = -\frac{\cancel{20}^{10}}{1} \cdot \frac{1}{\cancel{2}} = -\frac{10}{1} = -10$$

$$5\frac{1}{4} \cdot 1\frac{2}{7} \div 1\frac{1}{2} = \frac{21}{4} \cdot \frac{9}{7} \div \frac{3}{2} = \frac{\cancel{21}^{3}}{\cancel{4}_{2}} \cdot \frac{\cancel{9}^{3}}{\cancel{7}_{1}} \cdot \frac{\cancel{2}^{1}}{\cancel{3}_{1}} = \frac{9}{2} \text{ or } 4\frac{1}{2}$$

1. $-1\frac{2}{3} \cdot -3\frac{1}{5}$

2. $4\frac{5}{9} \div -\frac{10}{27}$

3. $4\frac{1}{4} \cdot 3\frac{1}{5}$

4. $-9\frac{3}{8} \div -3\frac{9}{12}$

5. $-\frac{3}{8} \cdot 4 \cdot \frac{4}{9}$

6. $-9\frac{3}{5} \div \frac{12}{5} \cdot -4$

7. $-4.1 \cdot -5.2 \div 4$

8. $6.2 \cdot 3 \cdot -\frac{1}{2}$
   (Hint: $\frac{1}{2} = .5$)

9. $(-2\frac{1}{2})(-2\frac{1}{2}) \div .5$

10. $-\frac{6}{7} \cdot -\frac{5}{12} \cdot -\frac{2}{15}$

11. $5\frac{2}{3} \cdot 9.81 \cdot 0$

12. $12 \cdot 3\frac{1}{4} \cdot -2\frac{2}{3}$

## ...More Multiplying and Dividing Rational Numbers

1. $-9 \frac{3}{5} \cdot \frac{5}{12}$

2. $-\frac{16}{7} \div \frac{12}{35}$

3. $4 \frac{1}{2} \cdot -2 \frac{2}{7}$

4. $-5 \frac{5}{6} \div 2 \frac{1}{3}$

5. $-8 \frac{1}{3} \cdot -2 \frac{2}{5}$

6. $16 \frac{1}{8} \div 14 \frac{1}{3}$

7. $-37.6 \cdot .03$

8. $-16.188 \div -4.26$

9. $-1.75 \cdot -3.4$

10. $-3.45 \div 1 \frac{1}{2}$

11. $-8 \div -1 \frac{1}{3} \cdot -5$

12. $4.498 \div -1.73 \cdot -1.2$

13. $-\frac{5}{7} \div -\frac{1}{14} \cdot -\frac{1}{2}$

14. $-6 \frac{2}{3} \cdot 2.75 \div -1 \frac{2}{3}$

15. $-\frac{3}{8} \div -3 \cdot \frac{4}{5}$

16. $12 \frac{3}{8} \cdot -2 \frac{2}{3} \div 2.5$

17. $-\frac{5}{6} \cdot 4 \frac{1}{4} \cdot -\frac{3}{5}$

18. $-3 \frac{1}{5} \div 4 \frac{2}{5} \div -1 \frac{1}{7}$

19. $3 \frac{3}{5} \cdot -1.46$

20. $4 \frac{2}{3} \div -\frac{6}{7} \cdot \frac{9}{10}$

# Rational Numbers

## Order of Operations with Rational Numbers

$$-3 \cdot 5 + 2 = -15 + 2 = -13$$

$$2\frac{1}{2} \div (5 + 5) = \frac{5}{2} \div 10 = \frac{\overset{1}{\cancel{5}}}{2} \cdot \frac{1}{\underset{2}{\cancel{10}}} = \frac{1}{4}$$

1. $-28 \div 7 + 2\frac{1}{3}$

2. $\frac{1}{2}(-16 - 4)$

3. $-9 \div -3 + 4 \cdot -\frac{1}{4} - 20 \div 5$

4. $\frac{1}{3}((-18 + 3) + (5 + 7) \div -4)$

5. $(8\frac{1}{3} + 3\frac{2}{3}) \div 4 - -16$

6. $\dfrac{(80 \cdot \frac{1}{2}) + 35}{-10 + 25}$

7. $2(-6(3 - 12) - 17)$

8. $\frac{1}{4}(20 + 72 \div -9)$

9. $3 \cdot 2(4 + (9 \div 3))$

10. $50 \div ((4 \cdot 5) - (36 \div 2)) + -91$

## ...More Order of Operations with Rational Numbers

1. $2 + (48 \div (12 + 4)) - 16$

2. $72 \div \left( \dfrac{29 + 7}{4 \cdot 3} \right) - (-26 + 92)$

3. $\left( \dfrac{3(12 - 7)}{2 + 3} \right) \cdot 6 + 11$

4. $\dfrac{2((7 \cdot 3) + 6)}{26 \div 13} - 8$

5. $\dfrac{5 + (4 \cdot 3(2 + 1)) + 4}{19 + -10}$

6. $\dfrac{((48 + 2)\,2) \div 5}{2} + 16$

7. $-16 + (20 \cdot 6) \div (6 + 2) + 31$

8. $\dfrac{7(8 - 1) + (42 \div 3)}{(10 - 7)\,3} + 7$

9. $35 + \dfrac{50 + 25}{5 \cdot 5} - (8 + 11)$

10. $(5(20 - 2)) \div \dfrac{30}{2} + 6 - 3$

11. $\dfrac{3(4(9 - 2))}{12} + (16 \cdot 3)$

12. $\left( \dfrac{(8 + 3) \cdot (16 - 7)}{3} + 11 \right) \div 4 + 8$

## Comparing Rational Numbers

Use <, > or = to make a true sentence.

$$5.68 \underline{\hspace{1cm}} 5.7 \qquad -7\frac{3}{10} \underline{\hspace{1cm}} -7.29$$
$$5.68 \quad < \quad 5.70 \qquad -7.30 \quad < \quad -7.29$$

1. $2.5 \underline{\hspace{1cm}} 2\frac{17}{34}$

2. $1.049 \underline{\hspace{1cm}} 1.49$

3. $-.\overline{3} \underline{\hspace{1cm}} -.3$

4. $15.62 \underline{\hspace{1cm}} 1.562$

5. $8156.6 \underline{\hspace{1cm}} 8166.6$

6. $-7\frac{4}{5} \underline{\hspace{1cm}} -7\frac{24}{30}$

7. $-8\frac{7}{8} \underline{\hspace{1cm}} -8.857$

8. $329.93 \underline{\hspace{1cm}} 32.993$

9. $982.61 \underline{\hspace{1cm}} 7662.8$

10. $13\frac{5}{8} \underline{\hspace{1cm}} 13.6$

Write in descending order.

$$5\frac{1}{2}, 5\frac{3}{5}, 5.4 \qquad 5.5, 5.6, 5.4 \qquad 5\frac{3}{5}, 5\frac{1}{2}, 5.4$$

Rewrite → Descending Order

1. $6.41, 6.411, 6.4111$

2. $-2\frac{9}{14}, -2\frac{5}{8}, -2\frac{4}{7}$

3. $11.6, 11\frac{2}{3}, 11\frac{14}{25}$

4. $-.030, -\frac{33}{100}, -.003$

5. $7\frac{5}{8}, 7\frac{3}{4}, 7.775$

6. $-10\frac{3}{4}, -10.82, -10\frac{2}{3}$

7. $3.08, 3\frac{4}{5}, 3\frac{3}{5}$

8. $-1.35, -1\frac{1}{8}, -1\frac{1}{4}$

## The Flip Tip

Perform each of the following operations on your calculator. Then flip your calculator and find the "word answer" to the questions.

1. What did Amelia Earhart's father say the first time he saw her fly an airplane?

    .115 x 3 + 10141 x 5 = _____

    Flip Tip _____

2. What did Farmer MacGregor throw at Peter Rabbit to chase him out of the garden?

    (27 x 109 + 4 − .027) 2 x 9 = _____

    Flip Tip _____

3. What did Snoopy add to his doghouse as a result of his dogfights with the Red Baron?

    7 (3 x 303 + 50 ) x 8 = _____

    Flip Tip _____

4. What kind of double does a golfer want to avoid at the end of a round of golf?

    4 (1956 x 4 + 153) = _____

    Flip Tip _____

5. What did the little girl say when she was frightened by the ghost?

    .07 x .111 x 5 + .00123 = _____

    Flip Tip _____

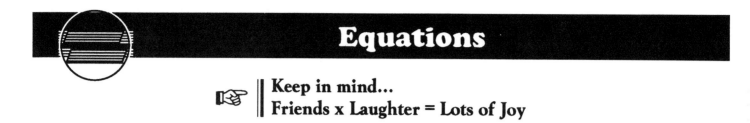

# Equations

☞ **Keep in mind...**
**Friends x Laughter = Lots of Joy**

## Open Sentences

State the solution for each sentence.

$$\frac{1}{2} \cdot -10 = x \qquad\qquad \frac{-56}{-7} - 4 = z$$

$$\frac{1}{\underset{1}{2}} \cdot \frac{\overset{-5}{\cancel{-10}}}{1} = x \qquad\qquad 8 - 4 = z$$

$$-5 = x \qquad\qquad 4 = z$$

1. $\dfrac{18 + -6}{2} = a$

2. $-3 \cdot 4 - 6 = c$

3. $4.5 - 6.2 = p$

4. $\dfrac{-3}{8} \cdot -4 - 1 = q$

5. $\dfrac{-15 + -27}{3} = x$

6. $-8.1 \cdot 4.2 + 16 = g$

7. $\dfrac{1}{3} \cdot -15 + -10 = r$

8. $1\dfrac{3}{5} \div \dfrac{16}{45} = d$

9. $5 \cdot 7.32 - 18.19 = n$

10. $\dfrac{3}{4} \cdot -16 + 8.12 = z$

11. $\dfrac{-40 + 15}{5} + 6 = b$

12. $-\dfrac{2}{5} \div \dfrac{4}{15} + -2\dfrac{1}{2} = t$

## ...More Open Sentences

Using the given value, state whether each problem is true or false.

$$28 = r \cdot \frac{1}{4}, \text{ if } r = \text{-}108$$

$$28 \overset{?}{=} \text{-}108 \cdot \frac{1}{4}$$

$$28 \overset{?}{=} \text{-}27 \Longrightarrow \text{False}$$

1. $7 + x = 3\frac{1}{2}$, if $x = \text{-}3\frac{1}{2}$

2. $y + 15 \div 6 = \text{-}1\frac{1}{2}$, if $y = \text{-}3$

3. $\frac{f}{13} + \text{-}3 = 0$, if $f = 69$

4. $2x - 5.45 = .97$, if $x = 3.21$

5. $8\frac{1}{3} + a = 15\frac{8}{15}$, if $a = 7\frac{2}{15}$

6. $8 + (z - 32) = \text{-}10$, if $z = 16$

7. $11.5 + c = 28\frac{1}{4}$, if $c = 16\frac{3}{4}$

8. $y(5 + 11) + 8 = 41$, if $y = 2$

9. $3g + 5.26 - 11.9 = 12.64$, if $g = \text{-}3$

10. $5 + \text{-}\frac{16}{k} = \text{-}3$, if $k = 2$

11. $7\frac{1}{9} \div w = \frac{1}{18}$, if $w = 2\frac{17}{32}$

12. $\frac{(2q - q)\,3}{8} + 29 = 32$, if $q = 8$

13. $\frac{16.8 - 91.6}{m} = 37.4$, if $m = 2$

14. $11\frac{1}{4} - f = 5\frac{1}{16}$, if $f = 16\frac{5}{16}$

## Evaluating Expressions

Evaluate the following, if $a = \frac{1}{2}$, $x = 4$ and $y = -2$.

$$5x \, (2a - 5y) = 5 \cdot 4 \, (2 \cdot \tfrac{1}{2} - 5 \cdot -2) = 20 \, (1 + 10) = 20 \, (11) = 220$$

1.  $4 \, (a - 1)$

2.  $4a - 3y$

3.  $4 \, (x - 3y)$

4.  $x \, (a + 6)$

5.  $6a + -12a$

6.  $7(x + -y)$

7.  $6a \, (8a + 4y)$

8.  $3x + 2(a - y)$

9.  $x \, (ax + ay)$

10.  $ay + y - 5ax$

11.  $xy \, (2a + 3x - 2)$

12.  $4x - (xy + 2)$

13.  $5y - 8a + 6xy - 7x$

14.  $10x \, (8a + -4y) + -3y$

15.  $6xy - 2x \, (4a - 8y)$

16.  $(2a - x) \, (2x - 6)$

## Simplifying Expressions

Distributive Property

$$3(x + 2y) = 3x + 3 \cdot 2y$$
$$= 3x + 6y$$

1. $-7(a + b)$

2. $x(y - 4)$

3. $-\frac{2}{3}(c - 12)$

4. $-8(\frac{t}{2} + 6)$

5. $y(-16 + 2x)$

6. $3(2a - 8b)$

7. $2x(3y + -6)$

8. $7(-5x + 8z)$

9. $-5y(6z - 10)$

10. $-3x(-7 + 8y)$

Combining Like Terms

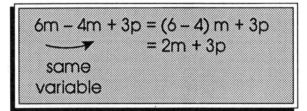

$$6m - 4m + 3p = (6 - 4)m + 3p$$
$$= 2m + 3p$$
same
variable

1. $9y + 6y - 2$

2. $25x - x + 2y$

3. $4a + 8b + 11a - 10b$

4. $13xy + 18xy - 20xy$

5. $-2m + 16 - 13m$

6. $4a + 7 + 3a - 8 - 3a$

7. $16x + -18y + 10x - 7y$

8. $6c - 8ab + 9c - 10$

9. $18ab + -6a + -7b + 26ab + -7b$

10. $5x - 3x + 2xy + 31x + -18xy$

## Mixed Practice

1. $3(a + b) + 2b$

2. $6m + 7(7m + 9)$

3. $5c + 2c(5 - 6)$

4. $8 - 3(6 - 6x)$

5. $4y + 6(y + 8)$

6. $3(d + 2e) - 11d$

7. $4a + -7(a + 2) + 13$

8. $6(i + 2j) + 8i - 16j$

9. $3ab + -2(a + b)$

10. $-6z(3 + 2y) + 8z$

11. $16d + -42e + 29de + 31e$

12. $-4k(2i + 3) + -6ki + 8k$

13. $-6x - 2(-5x + 9) - 3x$

14. $-17j + 8m(2 + 7n) + 7j$

15. $-3a - 2b(a + 8) - 6ab + 31b$

16. $2(2c + 11d) + 8c - 14d + -3cd$

17. $8(6z + 7y) - 11(2y + 8z)$

18. $14h + -16 - -7j + 8 + -11h$

19. $12d - -2d(8 + 6e) + 11de$

20. $4(11m - -8n) - 7(6n - 8p)$

21. $21s + -8t(-5s - 6) + 21st$

22. $-6(f + 5g) + -3(-7g - 11f)$

## Solving Addition Equations

$$1.8 = -2.1 + x$$
$$1.8 + 2.1 = -2.1 + 2.1 + x$$
$$3.9 = 0 + x$$
$$3.9 = x$$

1. $a + -7 = 8$

2. $y + 76 = -93$

3. $4 + b = -14$

4. $-33 = z + 16$

5. $-12 + x = 21$

6. $2.4 = m + 3.7$

7. $-1\frac{1}{2} + n = -1\frac{5}{8}$

8. $-27 = c + 27$

9. $-\frac{5}{8} + x = -\frac{5}{8}$

10. $y + -6.2 = 8.1$

11. $38 = x + -19$

12. $a + -2\frac{5}{9} = -10\frac{5}{18}$

13. $-1,129 + b = 3,331$

14. $-3.5 = 7\frac{1}{2} + x$

## Solving Subtraction Equations

$$24 = x - \text{-}8$$
$$24 = x + 8$$
$$24 - 8 = x + 8 - 8$$
$$16 = x + 0$$
$$16 = x$$

1. $k - 36 = 37$

2. $-22 = y - 8$

3. $x - \text{-}7 = -19$

4. $30 = b - \text{-}2$

5. $a - 18 = -32$

6. $-1.7 = b - 9.3$

7. $-4\frac{1}{3} = q - 3\frac{1}{3}$

8. $-17 = q - 3$

9. $p - \frac{3}{5} = \frac{3}{5}$

10. $5.62 = m - 6$

11. $x - \text{-}36.5 = -2.563$

12. $-1,132 = b - 6,339$

13. $7\frac{3}{4} = a - 16\frac{3}{16}$

14. $z - \text{-}5.75 = -8\frac{1}{4}$

## Solving Addition and Subtraction Equations

1. $x + -3 = -18$

2. $c - 11 = 43$

3. $12 + y = 32$

4. $-26 = d - 7$

5. $-62 = a + 16$

6. $q - -83 = 121$

7. $t + -101 = 263$

8. $w - 454 = -832$

9. $-332 = -129 + s$

10. $665 = k - -327$

11. $-8.6 = m + 11.12$

12. $a - -\frac{1}{5} = \frac{3}{20}$

13. $-\frac{3}{4} + z = \frac{7}{18}$

14. $b - 17.8 = -36$

15. $-\frac{13}{24} = -\frac{5}{16} + c$

16. $102.8 = g - -66.09$

17. $f + \frac{3}{5} = \frac{3}{4}$

18. $b - \frac{5}{6} = -\frac{7}{8}$

19. $21.21 + p = -101.6$

20. $-762.46 = h - 32.061$

# Equations

## Solving Multiplication Equations

$$4y = -28$$
$$\frac{4y}{4} = \frac{-28}{4}$$
$$1y = -7$$
$$y = -7$$

1. $-6a = -66$

2. $-180 = 12b$

3. $-13n = 13$

4. $42 = -14p$

5. $1\frac{1}{2} = 3x$

6. $-5.6 = -.8x$

7. $8 = -32b$

8. $9a = -3$

9. $.25y = 1.5$

10. $-.0006 = .02x$

11. $-11x = 275$

12. $45\frac{1}{2} = -14c$

13. $61.44 = 12z$

14. $-21y = -756$

## Solving Division Equations

$$\frac{x}{4} = -6$$

$$4 \cdot \frac{x}{4} = -6 \cdot 4$$

$$x = -24$$

1. $-18 = \frac{a}{6}$

2. $\frac{x}{6} = -6$

3. $\frac{y}{-2} = 231$

4. $\frac{1}{5} b = -8$

5. $\frac{m}{.6} = .3$

6. $35 = \frac{x}{-7}$

7. $.12 = \frac{y}{.12}$

8. $3 = -\frac{1}{8} a$

9. $\frac{w}{-2} = .04$

10. $\frac{u}{-4} = -14$

11. $\frac{x}{-5.1} = -16$

12. $-28 = \frac{a}{13}$

13. $\frac{1}{18} c = -31$

14. $\frac{b}{-.29} = 5.5$

## Solving Multiplication and Division Equations

1.  $-2p = -38$

2.  $\dfrac{b}{8} = -24$

3.  $-85 = 17r$

4.  $-32 = \dfrac{c}{-22}$

5.  $-13a = 52$

6.  $\dfrac{1}{47}d = -26$

7.  $-12f = -180$

8.  $\dfrac{i}{.16} = .7$

9.  $-77.4 = 9a$

10. $-\dfrac{1}{6}q = -11$

11. $16 = \dfrac{n}{-21}$

12. $.7h = -.112$

13. $-80 = \dfrac{p}{15}$

14. $792 = -33y$

15. $-5.2 = \dfrac{m}{30.1}$

16. $-11.2x = -60.48$

17. $\dfrac{1}{-26}r = -66$

18. $315 = 21s$

19. $\dfrac{z}{.06} = -7.98$

20. $-14g = -406$

## Mixed Practice with Equations

1.  $x + 12 = 8$

2.  $\dfrac{y}{-6} = 2$

3.  $-10 = m - 6$

4.  $2.7 = 3y$

5.  $-1 = \dfrac{r}{20}$

6.  $15 + a = -8$

7.  $-7b = -84$

8.  $-23 + w = 48$

9.  $9 = 54m$

10. $\dfrac{1}{16}x = 8$

11. $-42 = y - 20$

12. $92 + x = 92$

13. $2.5 = \dfrac{a}{.5}$

14. $-84 = 58 + a$

15. $a - {-163} = -292$

16. $-18.6 = -21s$

17. $-119 = x - 629$

18. $14.3m = -97.24$

19. $15.3 = z - {-29.23}$

20. $\dfrac{1}{18}y = -11$

## Solving Equations with 2 Operations

$$2y - 7 = -29$$
$$2y - 7 + 7 = -29 + 7$$
$$2y = -22$$
$$\frac{2y}{2} = \frac{-22}{2}$$
$$y = -11$$

1. $13 + -3p = -2$

2. $\dfrac{-5a}{2} = 75$

3. $6x - 4 = -10$

4. $9 = 2y + 9$

5. $-10 + \dfrac{a}{4} = 9$

6. $17 = 5 - x$

7. $-7r - 8 = -14$

8. $\dfrac{4y}{3} = 8$

9. $16 + \dfrac{x}{3} = -10$

10. $\dfrac{-4z}{5} = -12$

11. $-22 = 3s - -8$

12. $-\dfrac{a}{6} - -31 = 64$

## Solving Equations with Negative Variables

$$\frac{-k}{6} + 1 = -5$$

$$\frac{-k}{6} + 1 - 1 = -5 - 1$$

$$\frac{-k}{6} = -6$$

$$-6 \cdot \frac{-k}{6} = -6 \cdot -6$$

$$k = 36$$

1. $-8 - y = 22$

2. $18 = -k + 3$

3. $4 - \frac{x}{5} = -16$

4. $-x - 15 = -15$

5. $-z = 11$

6. $-28 = \frac{-y}{4} - 12$

7. $-82 = -a$

8. $\frac{-b}{3} + 50 = 100$

9. $-6 - x\frac{1}{9} = -18$

10. $-3z + 5 = 38$

11. $-a\frac{1}{2} + 12 = -9$

12. $-5y - -7 = 52$

## Mixed Practice

1.  $2x + 10 = 56$

2.  $-3a - 12 = 12$

3.  $7z - 13 = 15$

4.  $-11c + 10 = -45$

5.  $\dfrac{-f}{4} + 7 = -6$

6.  $2 + 5m = -18$

7.  $\dfrac{h}{-3} + 19 = 8$

8.  $75 = \dfrac{-5a}{3}$

9.  $5r - 6 = 29$

10. $-3 = -31 + \dfrac{c}{6}$

11. $\dfrac{-g}{12} - 4 = 7$

12. $9 - 4z = 57$

13. $\dfrac{4p}{-3} = 16$

14. $13 + \dfrac{p}{-3} = -4$

15. $-12 + \dfrac{j}{4} = 9$

16. $8 = \dfrac{h}{-3} + 19$

17. $\dfrac{t}{-9} + 60 = 47$

18. $\dfrac{-7k}{-4} = 35$

19. $-64 = 5y - 9$

20. $\dfrac{k}{5} + 36 = -51$

## Solving Equations Using the Distributive Property

$$4(x - 3) = 20$$
$$4x - 12 = 20$$
$$4x - 12 + 12 = 20 + 12$$
$$\frac{4x}{4} = \frac{32}{4}$$
$$x = 8$$

1.  $3(x + 8) = -6$

7.  $6(2 - \frac{x}{6}) = 1$

2.  $75 = -5(a + 5)$

8.  $-36 = 6(y - 2)$

3.  $-8(y - 6) = -16$

9.  $-7(r + 8) = -14$

4.  $20 = 4(\frac{t}{4} - 2)$

10.  $3(m + 5) = 42$

5.  $17(x - 2) = -34$

11.  $-54 = 3(2 + 5m)$

6.  $63 = 9(2 - a)$

12.  $-3(x - 7) + 2 = 20$

## Solving Equations—Variables on Both Sides

$$5x + 6 = 2x + 15$$
$$5x - 2x + 6 = 2x - 2x + 15$$
$$3x + 6 = 15$$
$$3x + 6 - 6 = 15 - 6$$
$$\frac{3x}{3} = \frac{9}{3}$$
$$x = 3$$

1. $20y + 5 = 5y + 65$

2. $13 - t = t - 7$

3. $-3k + 10 = k + 2$

4. $-9r = 20 + r$

5. $6m - 2\frac{1}{2} = m + 12\frac{1}{2}$

6. $18 + 4.5p = 6p + 12$

7. $5x - \frac{1}{4} = 3x - \frac{5}{4}$

8. $-x - 2 = 1 - 2x$

9. $3k + 10 = 2k - 21$

10. $8y - 6 = 5y + 12$

11. $-t + 10 = t + 4$

12. $4m - 9 = 5m + 7$

## Mixed Practice

1. $4x - 7 = 2x + 15$

2. $-4 = -4(f - 7)$

3. $5x - 17 = 4x + 36$

4. $3(k + 5) = -18$

5. $y + 3 = 7y - 21$

6. $-3(m - 2) = 12$

7. $18 + 4p = 6p + 12$

8. $-8(\frac{a}{8} - 2) = 26$

9. $-3k + 10 = k + 2$

10. $22 = 2(b + 3)$

11. $6a + 9 = -4a + 29$

12. $-22 = 11(2c + 8)$

13. $10p - 14 = 9p + 17$

14. $-45 = 5(\frac{2a}{5} + -3)$

15. $16z - 15 = 13z$

16. $36 + 19b = 24b + 6$

17. $144 = -16(3 + 3d)$

18. $11h - 14 = 7 + 14h$

19. $-3(\frac{2j}{3} - 6) = 32$

20. $-43 - 3z = 2 - 6z$

## ... More Mixed Practice

1.  $-116 = -a$

2.  $6m - 2 = m + 13$

3.  $4\left(\frac{x}{4} + 3\right) = -61$

4.  $-18 = -6 - y$

5.  $-5s + 16 = -59$

6.  $4a - 9 = 6a + 7$

7.  $-\frac{6b}{2} = -36$

8.  $-40 = 10(4 + s)$

9.  $28 - \frac{k}{3} = 16$

10. $-9r = 20 + r$

11. $114 = 11c - -26$

12. $-38 = 17 - 5z$

13. $-5(2x - 5) = -35$

14. $20c + 5 = 5c + 65$

15. $\frac{-d}{5} - 21 = -62$

16. $\frac{-15c}{-4} = -30$

17. $384 = 12(-8 + 5q)$

18. $3n + 7 = 7n - 13$

19. $-8 - \frac{z}{3} = 22$

20. $-6\left(\frac{5z}{6} + 5\right) = -60$

☞ **Keep in mind...**
**Tackle all your problems by taking them one at a time.**

## Writing Algebraic Expressions

| | |
|---|---|
| The product of four and 11 | $4 \cdot 11$ |
| A number increased by six | $x + 6$ |
| The number divided by two | $y + 2$ or $\frac{y}{2}$ |
| Twice a number decreased by one | $2a - 1$ |

1.   Five less than a number

2.   Three times the sum of a number and twelve

3.   Ten more than the quotient of c and three

4.   Two increased by six times a number

5.   Two-thirds of a number minus eleven

6.   Twice the difference between c and four

7.   The product of nine and a number, decreased by seven

8.   Six times a number plus seven times the number

9.   A number increased by twice the number

10.   One-fourth times a number increased by eleven

11.   The quotient of a number and three decreased by five

12.   Twelve times the sum of a number and five times the number

## Solving Problems...

Write an equation and solve.

> Nine more than a number is 33.
> Find the number.
> $9 + n = 33$
> $9 - 9 + n = 33 - 9$
> $n = 24$

1. A number decreased by 16 is -26. Find the number.

2. One-fourth of a number is -60. Find the number.

3. The product of negative eight and a number is 104. Find the number.

4. Twice a number is 346. Find the number.

5. A number increased by negative twenty-seven is 110. Find the number.

6. Tim weighs five pounds more than Mitchell. Find Mitchell's weight if Tim weighs ninety-three pounds.

7. The cost of five books is $71.00. What is the cost of each book?

8. The cost of a filter is $4.00. What is the cost of six filters?

## ...More Problems

Write an equation and solve.

> Ten more than 4 times a number is 6.
> What is the number?
> $10 + 4n = 6$
> $10 - 10 + 4n = 6 - 10$
> $\dfrac{4n}{4} = \dfrac{-4}{4}$
> $n = -1$

1.  Three-fifths of a number decreased by one is twenty-three. What is the number?

2.  Seven more than six times a number is negative forty-seven. What is the number?

3.  Nine less than twice a number is thirty-one. What is the number?

4.  Three times the sum of a number and five times the number is thirty-six. What is the number?

5.  The quotient of a number and four decreased by ten is two. What is the number?

6.  Carol is sixty-six inches tall. This is twenty inches less than two times Mindy's height. How tall is Mindy?

7.  In February, Paul's electric bill was three dollars more than one-half his gas bill. If the electric bill was ninety-two dollars, what was the gas bill?

## ...And More Problems

Write an equation and solve.

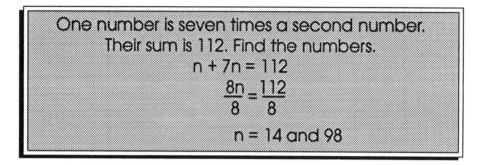

One number is seven times a second number.
Their sum is 112. Find the numbers.
$$n + 7n = 112$$
$$\frac{8n}{8} = \frac{112}{8}$$
$$n = 14 \text{ and } 98$$

1. One of two numbers is five more than the other. The sum of the numbers is 17. Find the numbers.

2. The sum of two numbers is twenty-four. The larger number is three times the smaller number. Find the numbers.

3. One of two numbers is two-thirds the other number. The sum of the numbers is 45. Find the numbers.

4. The difference of two numbers is 19. The larger number is 3 more than twice the smaller. Find the numbers.

5. 320 tickets were sold to the school play. There were 3 times as many student tickets sold as adult tickets. Find the number of each.

6. The first number is eight more than the second number. Three times the second number plus twice the first number is equal to 26. Find the numbers.

7. Dan has five times as many $1 bills as $5 bills. He has a total of 48 bills. How many of each does he have?

## ...And Still More Problems

Write an equation and solve.

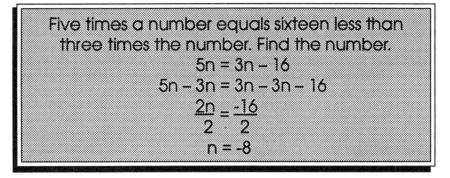

Five times a number equals sixteen less than
three times the number. Find the number.
$$5n = 3n - 16$$
$$5n - 3n = 3n - 3n - 16$$
$$\frac{2n}{2} = \frac{-16}{2}$$
$$n = -8$$

1.  Twenty decreased by twice a number is ten less than three times the number. Find the number.

2.  Half of a number is 18 more than 5 times the number. Find the number.

3.  Three times the sum of a number and twenty-one is twice the number increased by 23. Find the number.

4.  Twice a number decreased by 72 is five times the sum of the number and three times the number. Find the number.

5.  The length of a rectangle is 4 feet more than twice the width. Five times the width is the same as twice the length increased by 10 feet. Find the dimensions.

6.  Mike is 5 years older than David. Four times David's age increased by three years equals three times Mike's age decreased by two years. Find Mike's age.

7.  One board is one-third the length of another. Six times the sum of the length of the short board and -10 is equal to the length of the longer board decreased by 11 inches. Find the length of the longer board.

# Inequalities

☞ **Keep in mind...**
**You only fail when you stop trying.**

## Number Lines

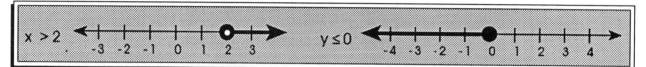

1.  $x > 1$

    ← | | | | | | | | | | | →
    -5  -4  -3  -2  -1  0  1  2  3  4  5

2.  $a < -1$

    ← | | | | | | | | | | | →
    -5  -4  -3  -2  -1  0  1  2  3  4  5

3.  $y \leq 2$

    ← | | | | | | | | | | | →
    -5  -4  -3  -2  -1  0  1  2  3  4  5

4.  $b > -4$

    ← | | | | | | | | | | | →
    -5  -4  -3  -2  -1  0  1  2  3  4  5

5.  $p \geq 3$

    ← | | | | | | | | | | | →
    -5  -4  -3  -2  -1  0  1  2  3  4  5

6.  $x < \frac{1}{2}$

    ← | | | | | | | | | | | →
    -5  -4  -3  -2  -1  0  1  2  3  4  5

7.  $y > -1.5$

    ← | | | | | | | | | | | →
    -5  -4  -3  -2  -1  0  1  2  3  4  5

8.  $m \leq 4\frac{1}{2}$

    ← | | | | | | | | | | | →
    -5  -4  -3  -2  -1  0  1  2  3  4  5

9.  $c \leq \frac{-11}{2}$

    ← | | | | | | | | | | | →
    -5  -4  -3  -2  -1  0  1  2  3  4  5

10. $d \geq 3.75$

    ← | | | | | | | | | | | →
    -5  -4  -3  -2  -1  0  1  2  3  4  5

## Solving Inequalities with Addition or Subtraction

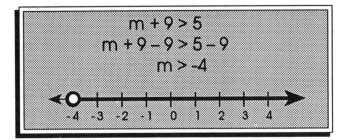

$$m + 9 > 5$$
$$m + 9 - 9 > 5 - 9$$
$$m > -4$$

1. $g + 8 > 6$

   -5 -4 -3 -2 -1 0 1 2 3 4 5

2. $d - 7 > -3$

   -5 -4 -3 -2 -1 0 1 2 3 4 5

3. $-3 > y + 1$

   -5 -4 -3 -2 -1 0 1 2 3 4 5

4. $a - 3 \leq 1$

   -5 -4 -3 -2 -1 0 1 2 3 4 5

5. $-4 \leq 1 + c$

   -5 -4 -3 -2 -1 0 1 2 3 4 5

6. $x + \frac{1}{4} \geq 1\frac{1}{2}$

   -5 -4 -3 -2 -1 0 1 2 3 4 5

7. $-2.4 < n - .6$

   -5 -4 -3 -2 -1 0 1 2 3 4 5

8. $-20 + m \leq -24$

   -5 -4 -3 -2 -1 0 1 2 3 4 5

9. $-7.5 + x \geq -9$

   -5 -4 -3 -2 -1 0 1 2 3 4 5

10. $3\frac{1}{3} \leq \frac{2}{9} + c$

   -5 -4 -3 -2 -1 0 1 2 3 4 5

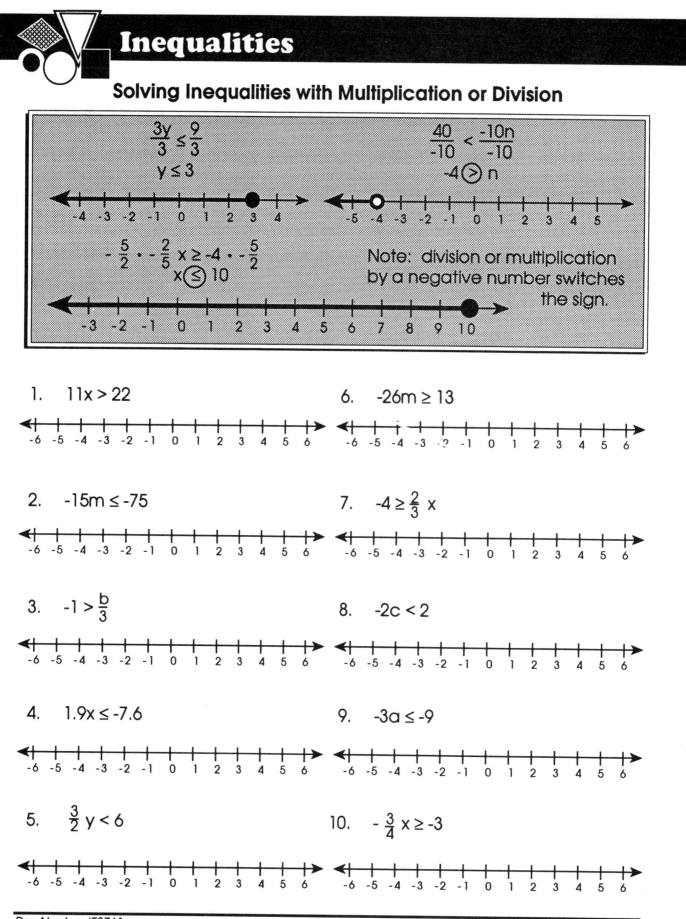

## Solving Inequalities with Multiplication or Division

$$\frac{3y}{3} \leq \frac{9}{3}$$
$$y \leq 3$$

$$\frac{40}{-10} < \frac{-10n}{-10}$$
$$-4 \circledgreater n$$

$$-\frac{5}{2} \cdot -\frac{2}{5}x \geq -4 \cdot -\frac{5}{2}$$
$$x \circledless 10$$

Note: division or multiplication by a negative number switches the sign.

1. $11x > 22$

2. $-15m \leq -75$

3. $-1 > \frac{b}{3}$

4. $1.9x \leq -7.6$

5. $\frac{3}{2}y < 6$

6. $-26m \geq 13$

7. $-4 \geq \frac{2}{3}x$

8. $-2c < 2$

9. $-3a \leq -9$

10. $-\frac{3}{4}x \geq -3$

## Mixed Practice

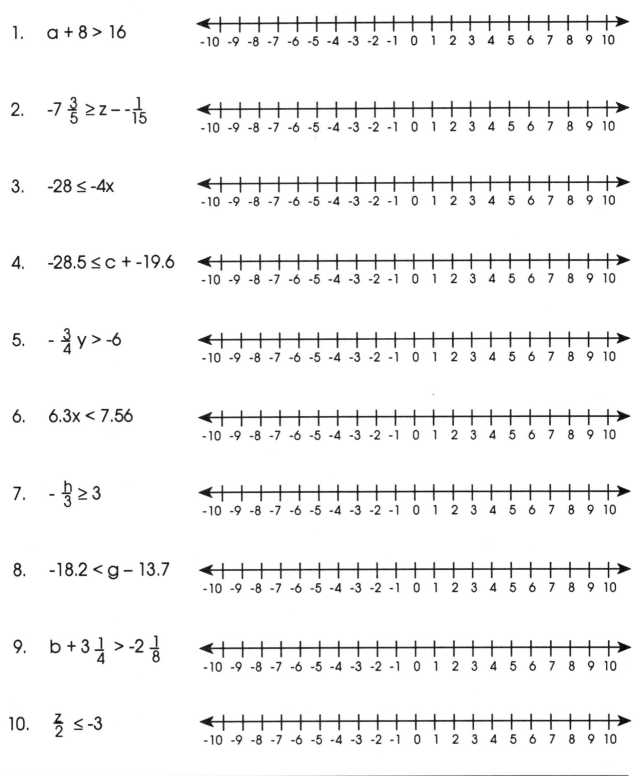

1.  $a + 8 > 16$

2.  $-7\frac{3}{5} \geq z - -\frac{1}{15}$

3.  $-28 \leq -4x$

4.  $-28.5 \leq c + -19.6$

5.  $-\frac{3}{4}y > -6$

6.  $6.3x < 7.56$

7.  $-\frac{h}{3} \geq 3$

8.  $-18.2 < g - 13.7$

9.  $b + 3\frac{1}{4} > -2\frac{1}{8}$

10. $\frac{z}{2} \leq -3$

# Inequalities

## Solving Inequalities with More Than One Operation

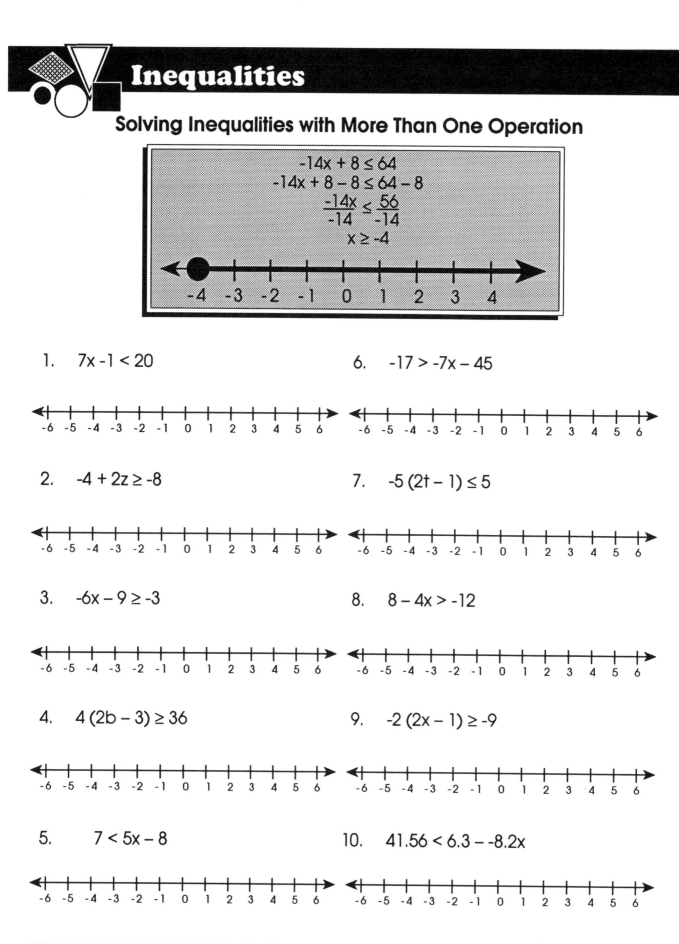

$-14x + 8 \le 64$

$-14x + 8 - 8 \le 64 - 8$

$\dfrac{-14x}{-14} \le \dfrac{56}{-14}$

$x \ge -4$

1.  $7x - 1 < 20$

6.  $-17 > -7x - 45$

2.  $-4 + 2z \ge -8$

7.  $-5(2t - 1) \le 5$

3.  $-6x - 9 \ge -3$

8.  $8 - 4x > -12$

4.  $4(2b - 3) \ge 36$

9.  $-2(2x - 1) \ge -9$

5.  $7 < 5x - 8$

10.  $41.56 < 6.3 - -8.2x$

## Solving Inequalities with Variables on Both Sides

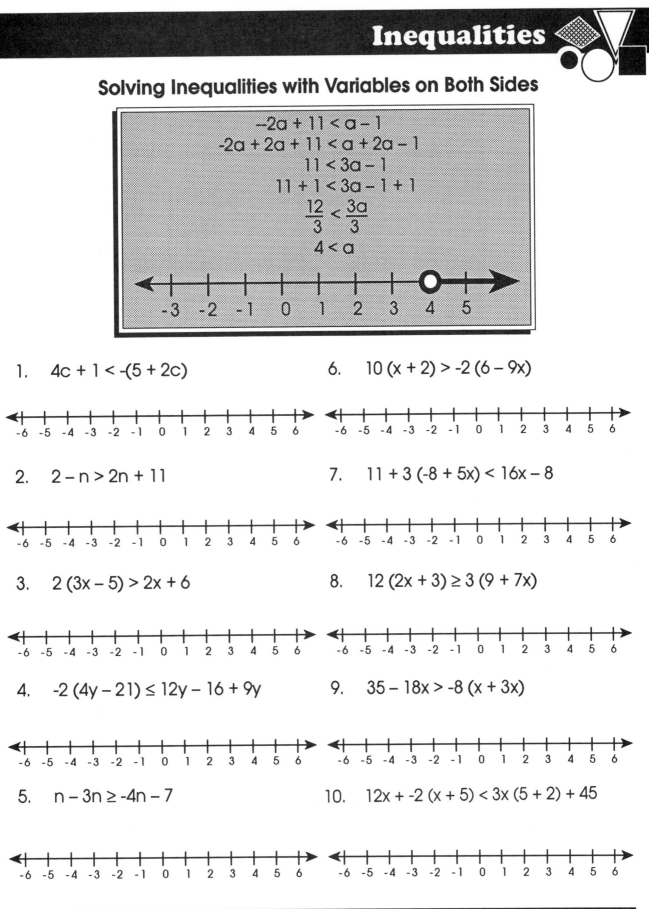

$-2a + 11 < a - 1$

$-2a + 2a + 11 < a + 2a - 1$

$11 < 3a - 1$

$11 + 1 < 3a - 1 + 1$

$\dfrac{12}{3} < \dfrac{3a}{3}$

$4 < a$

1. $4c + 1 < -(5 + 2c)$

2. $2 - n > 2n + 11$

3. $2(3x - 5) > 2x + 6$

4. $-2(4y - 21) \le 12y - 16 + 9y$

5. $n - 3n \ge -4n - 7$

6. $10(x + 2) > -2(6 - 9x)$

7. $11 + 3(-8 + 5x) < 16x - 8$

8. $12(2x + 3) \ge 3(9 + 7x)$

9. $35 - 18x > -8(x + 3x)$

10. $12x + -2(x + 5) < 3x(5 + 2) + 45$

## Mixed Practice with Inequalities

1. $32.4 \geq -6c$

-10 -9 -8 -7 -6 -5 -4 -3 -2 -1 0 1 2 3 4 5 6 7 8 9 10

2. $x - -15 \leq 9$

-10 -9 -8 -7 -6 -5 -4 -3 -2 -1 0 1 2 3 4 5 6 7 8 9 10

3. $-\frac{2}{3}b > -6$

-10 -9 -8 -7 -6 -5 -4 -3 -2 -1 0 1 2 3 4 5 6 7 8 9 10

4. $-18 + d > -11$

-10 -9 -8 -7 -6 -5 -4 -3 -2 -1 0 1 2 3 4 5 6 7 8 9 10

5. $6(2z + 3) \leq -54$

-10 -9 -8 -7 -6 -5 -4 -3 -2 -1 0 1 2 3 4 5 6 7 8 9 10

6. $8y - 15 < 27 + 2y$

-10 -9 -8 -7 -6 -5 -4 -3 -2 -1 0 1 2 3 4 5 6 7 8 9 10

7. $162 > -3a(5 + 1)$

-10 -9 -8 -7 -6 -5 -4 -3 -2 -1 0 1 2 3 4 5 6 7 8 9 10

8. $-6(5x + 8) \geq 2(8 - 7x)$

-10 -9 -8 -7 -6 -5 -4 -3 -2 -1 0 1 2 3 4 5 6 7 8 9 10

9. $-40 \leq 8(2t - 2)$

-10 -9 -8 -7 -6 -5 -4 -3 -2 -1 0 1 2 3 4 5 6 7 8 9 10

10. $5x(2 - 3) < 3x + 62$

-10 -9 -8 -7 -6 -5 -4 -3 -2 -1 0 1 2 3 4 5 6 7 8 9 10

## ...More Mixed Practice with Inequalities

1. $9x - 8 + x < 16 + 4x$

2. $15y \geq -45$

3. $69 > c + 71$

4. $17 + 11n - 13 \leq 4(n + 1) + 2n$

5. $8(2 + x) > 3(x - 3)$

6. $-4(3x + 2) \geq 40$

7. $\frac{5}{3} < \frac{2}{3}x - 1$

8. $3n - 4(2n - 5) + n + 4 \geq 0$

9. $18c + 11 - 26c < -3c(5 + 1) - 59$

10. $8a - 2(2a + 5) \leq 2a(9 + 1) + 54$

## A Logical Conclusion

Mike, Dale, Paul and Charlie are the athletic director, quarterback, pitcher and goalie, but not necessarily in that order. From these five statements, identify the man in each position.

1. Mike and Dale were both at the ball park when the rookie pitcher played his first game.

2. Both Paul and the athletic director had played on the same team in high school with the goalie.

3. The athletic director, who scouted Charlie, is planning to watch Mike during his next game.

4. Mike doesn't know Dale.

5. One of these men is a quarterback.

|  | Quarterback | Goalie | Pitcher | Athletic Director |
|---|---|---|---|---|
| Mike |  |  |  |  |
| Dale |  |  |  |  |
| Paul |  |  |  |  |
| Charlie |  |  |  |  |

☞ **Keep in mind...**
**Challenges make you discover things about yourself**
**that you never really knew.**

**– Cicely Tyson**

## Plotting Points

Connect each of the following ordered points.

(x, y) = (0, -1)
└─── vertical move ⟹ down one
└──── horizontal move ⟹ no move

"Ancient History"

Start at (0, -1)

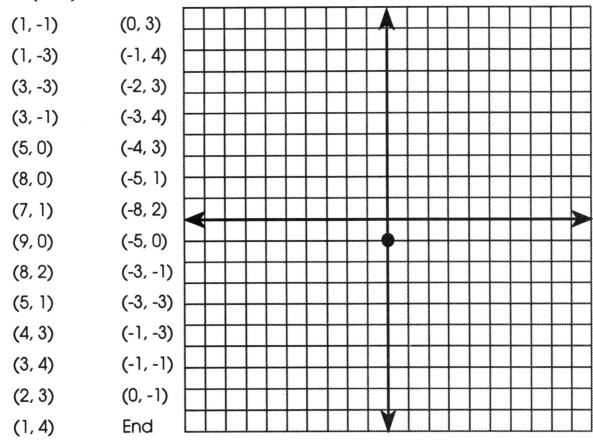

| | |
|---|---|
| (1, -1) | (0, 3) |
| (1, -3) | (-1, 4) |
| (3, -3) | (-2, 3) |
| (3, -1) | (-3, 4) |
| (5, 0) | (-4, 3) |
| (8, 0) | (-5, 1) |
| (7, 1) | (-8, 2) |
| (9, 0) | (-5, 0) |
| (8, 2) | (-3, -1) |
| (5, 1) | (-3, -3) |
| (4, 3) | (-1, -3) |
| (3, 4) | (-1, -1) |
| (2, 3) | (0, -1) |
| (1, 4) | End |

# Ordered Pairs and Graphing

## Coordinates and Graphing

Find the coordinates associated with the following points.

1. A
2. K
3. E
4. P
5. T

6. C
7. B
8. S
9. D
10. N

Find the letter associated with each pair of coordinates.

11. (2, 1)
12. (-1, -4)
13. (10, 3)
14. (7, -6)
15. (-2, -1)

16. (-2, 3)
17. (-3, 0)
18. (4, 4)
19. (-5, -2)
20. (0, -2)

## Solving for y

Solve each equation for y. Then use the given values for x to find the corresponding values for y. Write answers as ordered pairs.

$$y - 4 = 3x$$
$$y - 4 + 4 = 3x + 4$$
$$y = 3x + 4$$

Let x = -2, 0, 1
} Solve for y

a. $y = 3 \cdot -2 + 4$
$y = -6 + 4$
$y = -2$
(-2, -2)

b. $y = 3 \cdot 0 + 4$
$y = 0 + 4$
$y = 4$
(0, 4)

c. $y = 3 \cdot 1 + 4$
$y = 3 + 4$
$y = 7$
(1, 7)

1.  $y = 5x$      Let x = -3, 0, 2      Note: This equation is already in the form of y = ...

2.  $2x + y = 9$      Let x = -1, 0, 5

3.  $-x = y + 3$      Let x = -3, 0, 4

4.  $y = \frac{2}{3} x + 1$      Let x = -4, 0, 3

5.  $8x + y = 1$      Let x = -2, 0, 1

6.  $y - 1 = -3x$      Let x = -3, 0, 2

7.  $2 = y - \frac{1}{3} x$      Let x = -9, 0, 6

8.  $7x - y = -8$      Let x = -1, 0, -3

## Graphing Linear Equations by Plotting Points

Solve each equation for y. Then choose 3 values for x and find the corresponding values for y. Graph the 3 ordered pairs and draw the line that contains them.

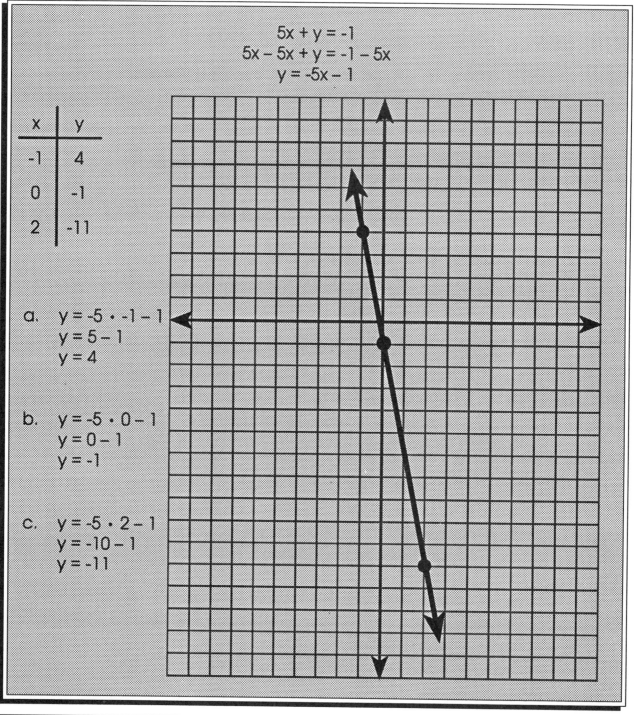

$$5x + y = -1$$
$$5x - 5x + y = -1 - 5x$$
$$y = -5x - 1$$

| x | y |
|---|---|
| -1 | 4 |
| 0 | -1 |
| 2 | -11 |

a.  $y = -5 \cdot -1 - 1$
    $y = 5 - 1$
    $y = 4$

b.  $y = -5 \cdot 0 - 1$
    $y = 0 - 1$
    $y = -1$

c.  $y = -5 \cdot 2 - 1$
    $y = -10 - 1$
    $y = -11$

1. $y = \frac{1}{2}x - 3$

5. $3x + y = 7$

2. $-2x + y = 5$

6. $3x - y = -2$

3. $4x + y = -7$

7. $y + 7 = 5x$

4. $y - 3 = 2x$

8. $y = \frac{1}{4}x - 2$

9.  $\frac{3}{4}x + y = 2$

13. $y = -\frac{1}{2}x$

10. $x - y = -4$

14. $\frac{1}{4}x + y = -2$

11. $-3x + y = -4$

15. $y = -4x - 5$

12. $y - x = -1$

16. $y = -2x - 3$

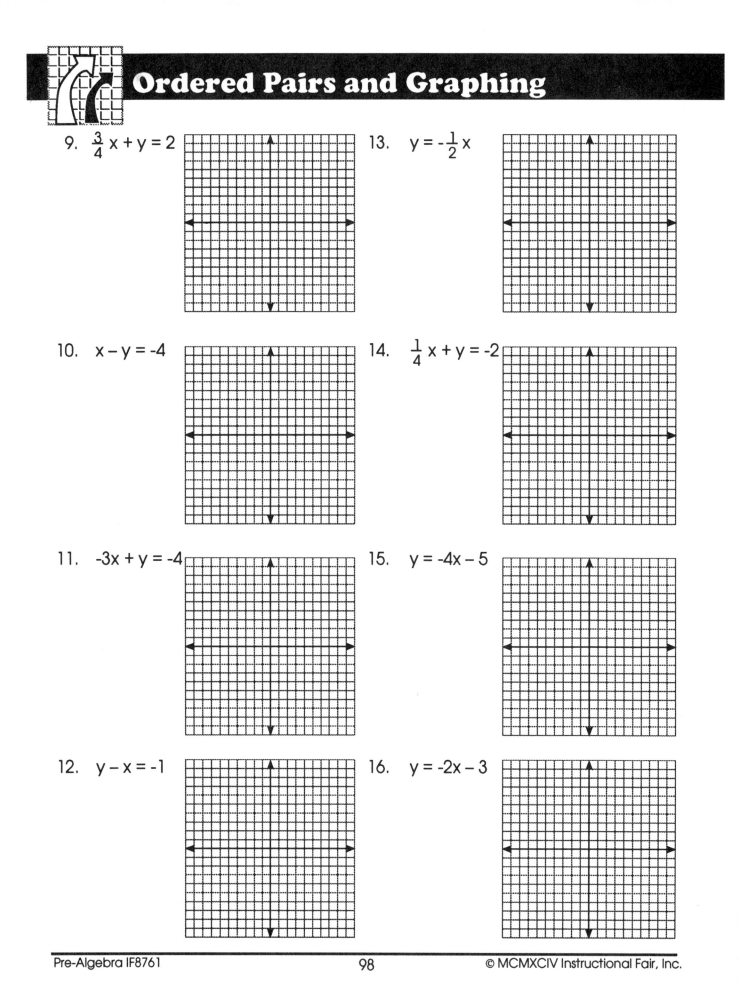

## Slope

Find the slope of the line passing through the given points.

I. Using the graph of the line

$$\text{slope} = \frac{\text{change in y}}{\text{change in x}}$$

Choose any 2 points to count the change.

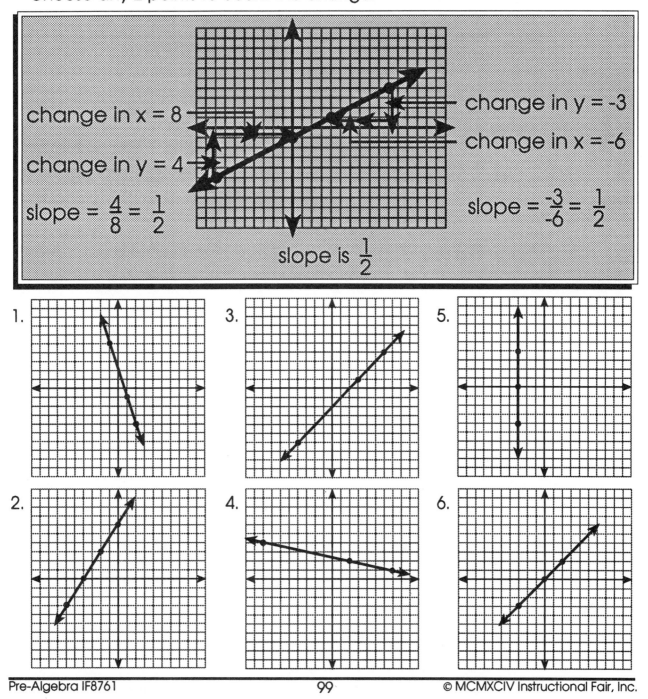

change in x = 8

change in y = 4

slope = $\frac{4}{8}$ = $\frac{1}{2}$

change in y = -3

change in x = -6

slope = $\frac{-3}{-6}$ = $\frac{1}{2}$

slope is $\frac{1}{2}$

1.

2.

3.

4.

5.

6.

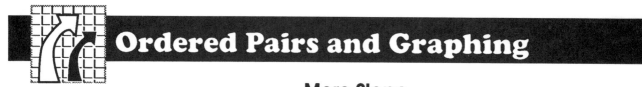

## ...More Slope

II. Using the formula

$$\text{slope} = \frac{\text{difference in y-values}}{\text{difference in x-values}}$$

> P (5, 3)    R (-1, 1)
>
> slope of PR = $\dfrac{3-1}{5-(-1)}$ = $\dfrac{2}{6}$ = $\dfrac{1}{3}$
>
> slope is $\dfrac{1}{3}$

1.  A (-3, 1)    D (4, 5)

2.  C (2, 6)    F (3, 5)

3.  B (0, 8)    G (3, 2)

4.  J (-6, -3)    K (-4, 5)

5.  P (9, 4)    M (7, 3)

6.  Q (0, -4)    R (1, -6)

7.  L (-2, 6)    N (2, -3)

8.  S (-1, -3)    X (2, -6)

9.  T (-4, -4)    Z (6, 3)

10. V $(\frac{3}{4}, \frac{3}{2})$    W $(\frac{11}{4}, \frac{5}{2})$

11. U (2, 3)    A (-2, 3)

12. C (4, -1)    D (-2, 2)

13. Z (3, 5)    H (5, 10)

14. J (-2, -3)    K (13, 7)

## Graphing Linear Equations Using Slope

Graph the line that contains the given point and has the given slope.

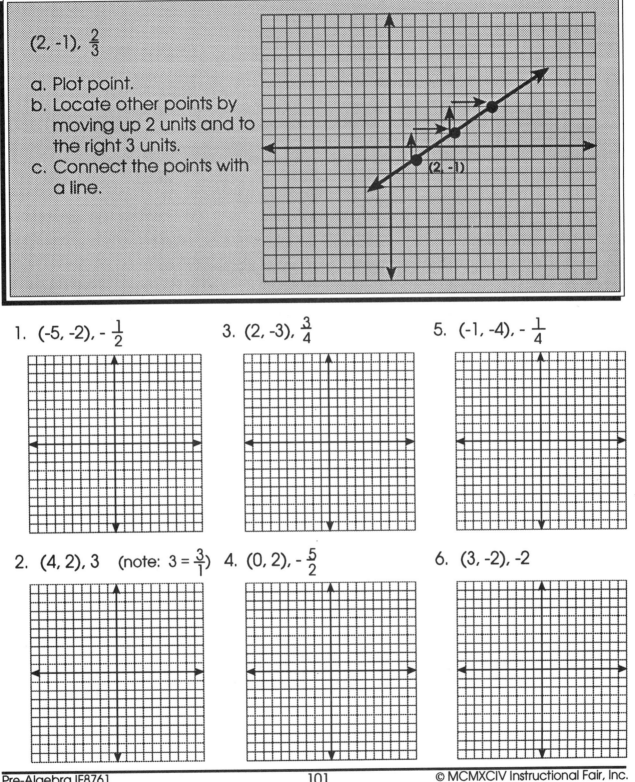

$(2, -1), \frac{2}{3}$

a. Plot point.
b. Locate other points by moving up 2 units and to the right 3 units.
c. Connect the points with a line.

(2, -1)

1.  $(-5, -2), -\frac{1}{2}$

3.  $(2, -3), \frac{3}{4}$

5.  $(-1, -4), -\frac{1}{4}$

2.  $(4, 2), 3$   (note: $3 = \frac{3}{1}$)

4.  $(0, 2), -\frac{5}{2}$

6.  $(3, -2), -2$

## Graphing Linear Equations Using y-Intercept and Slope

Graph the lines given the equation using the y-intercept and slope.

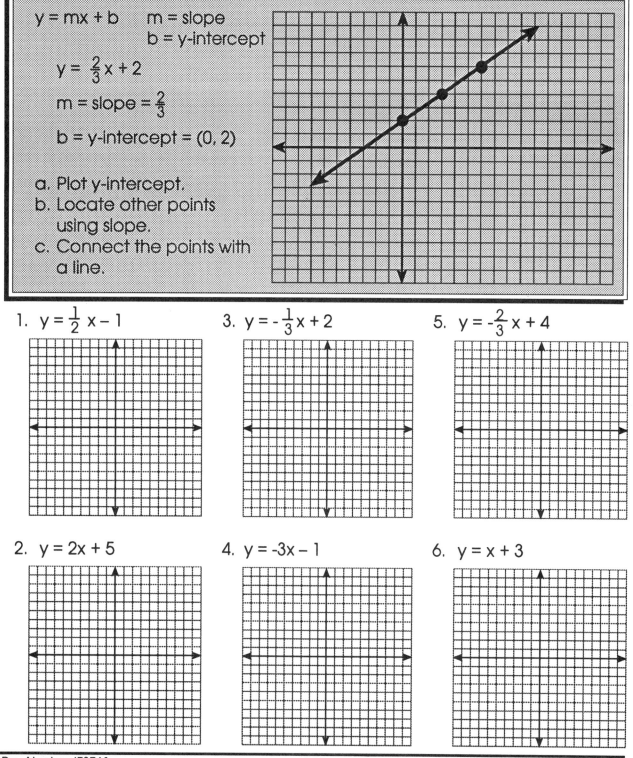

$y = mx + b$    $m$ = slope

$b$ = y-intercept

$y = \frac{2}{3}x + 2$

$m$ = slope = $\frac{2}{3}$

$b$ = y-intercept = $(0, 2)$

a. Plot y-intercept.
b. Locate other points using slope.
c. Connect the points with a line.

1. $y = \frac{1}{2}x - 1$

3. $y = -\frac{1}{3}x + 2$

5. $y = -\frac{2}{3}x + 4$

2. $y = 2x + 5$

4. $y = -3x - 1$

6. $y = x + 3$

# Answer Key

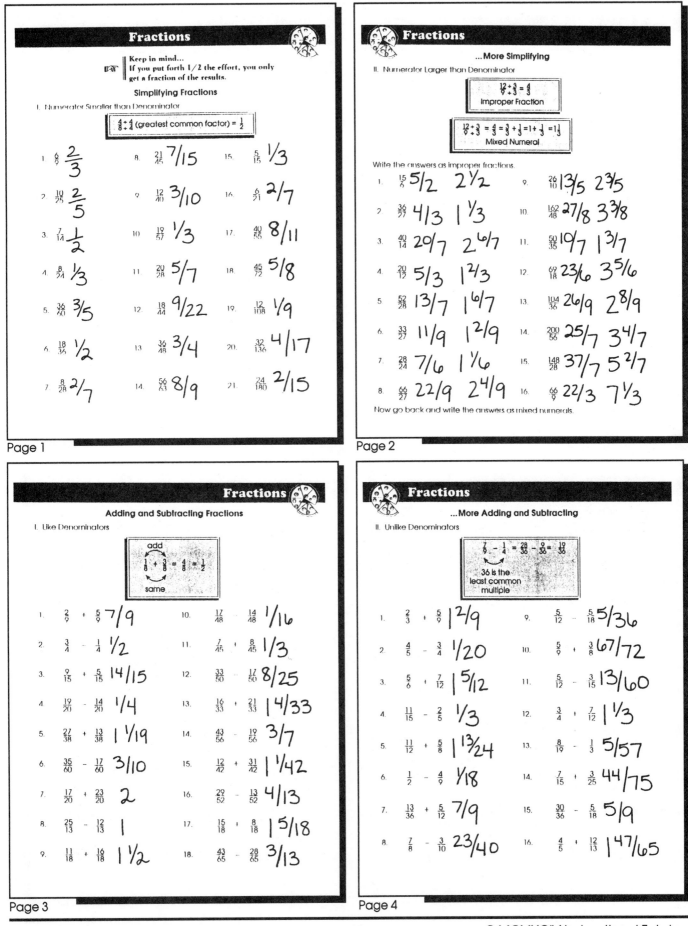

## Fractions

**Keep in mind...**
If you put forth 1/2 the effort, you only get a fraction of the results.

### Simplifying Fractions

I. Numerator Smaller than Denominator

$$\frac{4 \div 4}{8 \div 4} \text{ (greatest common factor)} = \frac{1}{2}$$

1. $\frac{6}{9}$  $\frac{2}{3}$
2. $\frac{10}{25}$  $\frac{2}{5}$
3. $\frac{7}{14}$  $\frac{1}{2}$
4. $\frac{8}{24}$  1/3
5. $\frac{36}{60}$  3/5
6. $\frac{18}{36}$  1/2
7. $\frac{8}{28}$  2/7

8. $\frac{21}{45}$  7/15
9. $\frac{12}{40}$  3/10
10. $\frac{19}{57}$  1/3
11. $\frac{20}{28}$  5/7
12. $\frac{18}{44}$  9/22
13. $\frac{36}{48}$  3/4
14. $\frac{56}{63}$  8/9

15. $\frac{5}{15}$  1/3
16. $\frac{6}{21}$  2/7
17. $\frac{40}{55}$  8/11
18. $\frac{45}{72}$  5/8
19. $\frac{12}{108}$  1/9
20. $\frac{32}{136}$  4/17
21. $\frac{24}{180}$  2/15

**Page 1**

## Fractions

### ...More Simplifying

II. Numerator Larger than Denominator

$$\frac{12 \div 3}{9 \div 3} = \frac{4}{3}$$
Improper Fraction

$$\frac{12 \div 3}{9 \div 3} = \frac{4}{3} = \frac{3}{3} + \frac{1}{3} = 1 + \frac{1}{3} = 1\frac{1}{3}$$
Mixed Numeral

Write the answers as improper fractions.

1. $\frac{15}{6}$  5/2  2½
2. $\frac{36}{27}$  4/3  1⅓
3. $\frac{40}{14}$  20/7  2⁶/7
4. $\frac{20}{12}$  5/3  1²/3
5. $\frac{52}{28}$  13/7  1⁶/7
6. $\frac{33}{27}$  11/9  1²/9
7. $\frac{28}{24}$  7/6  1⅙
8. $\frac{66}{27}$  22/9  2⁴/9

9. $\frac{26}{10}$  13/5  2³/5
10. $\frac{162}{48}$  27/8  3³/8
11. $\frac{50}{35}$  10/7  1³/7
12. $\frac{69}{18}$  23/6  3⁵/6
13. $\frac{104}{36}$  26/9  2⁸/9
14. $\frac{200}{56}$  25/7  3⁴/7
15. $\frac{148}{28}$  37/7  5²/7
16. $\frac{66}{9}$  22/3  7⅓

Now go back and write the answers as mixed numerals.

**Page 2**

## Fractions

### Adding and Subtracting Fractions

I. Like Denominators

add
$$\frac{1}{8} + \frac{3}{8} = \frac{4}{8} = \frac{1}{2}$$
same

1. $\frac{2}{9} + \frac{5}{9}$  7/9
2. $\frac{3}{4} - \frac{1}{4}$  ½
3. $\frac{9}{15} + \frac{5}{15}$  14/15
4. $\frac{19}{20} - \frac{14}{20}$  1/4
5. $\frac{27}{38} + \frac{13}{38}$  1 1/19
6. $\frac{35}{60} - \frac{17}{60}$  3/10
7. $\frac{17}{20} + \frac{23}{20}$  2
8. $\frac{25}{13} - \frac{12}{13}$  1
9. $\frac{11}{18} + \frac{16}{18}$  1½

10. $\frac{17}{48} - \frac{14}{48}$  1/16
11. $\frac{7}{45} + \frac{8}{45}$  1/3
12. $\frac{33}{50} - \frac{17}{50}$  8/25
13. $\frac{16}{33} + \frac{21}{33}$  1 4/33
14. $\frac{43}{56} - \frac{19}{56}$  3/7
15. $\frac{12}{42} + \frac{31}{42}$  1 1/42
16. $\frac{29}{52} - \frac{13}{52}$  4/13
17. $\frac{15}{18} + \frac{8}{18}$  1 5/18
18. $\frac{43}{65} - \frac{28}{65}$  3/13

**Page 3**

## Fractions

### ...More Adding and Subtracting

II. Unlike Denominators

$$\frac{7}{9} - \frac{1}{4} = \frac{28}{36} - \frac{9}{36} = \frac{19}{36}$$
36 is the least common multiple

1. $\frac{2}{3} + \frac{5}{9}$  1 2/9
2. $\frac{4}{5} - \frac{3}{4}$  1/20
3. $\frac{5}{6} + \frac{7}{12}$  1 5/12
4. $\frac{11}{15} - \frac{2}{5}$  1/3
5. $\frac{11}{12} + \frac{5}{8}$  1 13/24
6. $\frac{1}{2} - \frac{4}{9}$  1/18
7. $\frac{13}{36} + \frac{5}{12}$  7/9
8. $\frac{7}{8} - \frac{3}{10}$  23/40

9. $\frac{5}{12} - \frac{5}{18}$  5/36
10. $\frac{5}{9} + \frac{3}{8}$  67/72
11. $\frac{5}{12} - \frac{3}{15}$  13/60
12. $\frac{3}{4} + \frac{7}{12}$  1 1/3
13. $\frac{8}{19} - \frac{1}{3}$  5/57
14. $\frac{7}{15} + \frac{3}{25}$  44/75
15. $\frac{30}{36} - \frac{5}{18}$  5/9
16. $\frac{4}{5} + \frac{12}{13}$  1 47/65

**Page 4**

# Answer Key

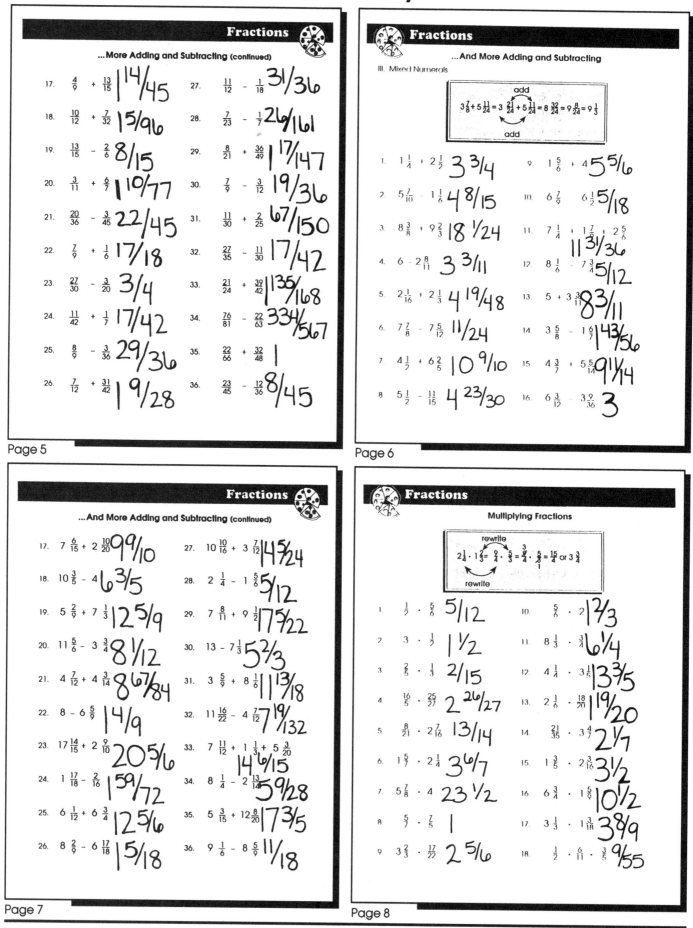

**Fractions**

### ...More Adding and Subtracting (continued)

17. $\frac{4}{9} + \frac{13}{15}$ = 1 14/45
18. $\frac{10}{12} + \frac{7}{32}$ = 15/96
19. $\frac{13}{15} - \frac{2}{6}$ = 8/15
20. $\frac{3}{11} + \frac{6}{7}$ = 1 10/77
21. $\frac{20}{36} - \frac{3}{45}$ = 22/45
22. $\frac{7}{9} + \frac{1}{6}$ = 17/18
23. $\frac{27}{30} - \frac{3}{20}$ = 3/4
24. $\frac{11}{42} + \frac{1}{7}$ = 17/42
25. $\frac{8}{9} - \frac{3}{36}$ = 29/36
26. $\frac{7}{12} + \frac{31}{42}$ = 1 9/28

27. $\frac{11}{12} - \frac{1}{18}$ = 31/36
28. $\frac{7}{23} - \frac{1}{7}$ = 26/161
29. $\frac{8}{21} + \frac{36}{49}$ = 1 17/147
30. $\frac{7}{9} - \frac{3}{12}$ = 19/36
31. $\frac{11}{30} + \frac{2}{25}$ = 67/150
32. $\frac{27}{35} - \frac{11}{30}$ = 17/42
33. $\frac{21}{24} + \frac{39}{42}$ = 1 35/168
34. $\frac{76}{81} - \frac{22}{63}$ = 334/567
35. $\frac{22}{66} + \frac{32}{48}$ = 1
36. $\frac{23}{45} - \frac{12}{36}$ = 8/45

Page 5

## Fractions

### ...And More Adding and Subtracting
III. Mixed Numerals

$$3\tfrac{7}{8} + 5\tfrac{11}{24} = 3\tfrac{21}{24} + 5\tfrac{11}{24} = 8\tfrac{32}{24} = 9\tfrac{8}{24} = 9\tfrac{1}{3}$$

1. $1\frac{1}{4} + 2\frac{1}{2}$ = 3 3/4
2. $5\frac{7}{10} - 1\frac{1}{6}$ = 4 8/15
3. $8\frac{3}{8} + 9\frac{2}{3}$ = 18 1/24
4. $6 - 2\frac{8}{11}$ = 3 3/11
5. $2\frac{1}{16} + 2\frac{1}{3}$ = 4 19/48
6. $7\frac{7}{8} - 7\frac{5}{12}$ = 11/24
7. $4\frac{1}{2} + 6\frac{2}{5}$ = 10 9/10
8. $5\frac{1}{2} - 1\frac{1}{15}$ = 4 23/30

9. $1\frac{5}{6} + 4$ = 5 5/6
10. $6\frac{7}{9} - 6\frac{1}{2}$ = 5/18
11. $7\frac{1}{4} + 1\frac{7}{9} + 2\frac{5}{6}$ = 11 31/36
12. $8\frac{1}{6} - 7\frac{3}{4}$ = 5/12
13. $5 + 3\frac{3}{11}$ = 8 3/11
14. $3\frac{5}{8} - 1\frac{6}{7}$ = 1 43/56
15. $4\frac{3}{7} + 5\frac{5}{14}$ = 9 11/14
16. $6\frac{3}{12} - 3\frac{9}{36}$ = 3

Page 6

## Fractions

### ...And More Adding and Subtracting (continued)

17. $7\frac{6}{15} + 2\frac{10}{20}$ = 9 9/10
18. $10\frac{3}{5} - 4$ = 6 3/5
19. $5\frac{2}{9} + 7\frac{1}{3}$ = 12 5/9
20. $11\frac{5}{6} - 3\frac{3}{4}$ = 8 1/12
21. $4\frac{7}{12} + 4\frac{3}{14}$ = 8 67/84
22. $8 - 6\frac{5}{9}$ = 1 4/9
23. $17\frac{14}{15} + 2\frac{9}{10}$ = 20 5/6
24. $1\frac{17}{18} - \frac{2}{16}$ = 1 59/72
25. $6\frac{1}{12} + 6\frac{3}{4}$ = 12 5/6
26. $8\frac{2}{9} - 6\frac{17}{18}$ = 1 5/18

27. $10\frac{10}{16} + 3\frac{7}{12}$ = 14 5/24
28. $2\frac{1}{4} - 1\frac{5}{6}$ = 5/12
29. $7\frac{8}{11} + 9\frac{1}{?}$ = 17 5/22
30. $13 - 7\frac{1}{3}$ = 5 2/3
31. $3\frac{5}{9} + 8\frac{1}{6}$ = 11 13/18
32. $11\frac{16}{22} - 4\frac{7}{12}$ = 7 19/132
33. $7\frac{1}{12} + 1\frac{1}{3} + 5\frac{3}{20}$ = 14 6/15
34. $8\frac{1}{4} - 2\frac{13}{14}$ = 5 9/28
35. $5\frac{3}{15} + 12\frac{8}{20}$ = 17 3/5
36. $9\frac{1}{6} - 8\frac{5}{9}$ = 11/18

Page 7

## Fractions

### Multiplying Fractions

$$2\tfrac{1}{4} \cdot 1\tfrac{2}{3} = \frac{9}{4} \cdot \frac{5}{3} = \frac{3 \cdot 5}{4 \cdot 1} = \frac{15}{4} \text{ or } 3\tfrac{3}{4}$$

1. $\frac{1}{2} \cdot \frac{5}{6}$ = 5/12
2. $3 \cdot \frac{1}{2}$ = 1 1/2
3. $\frac{2}{5} \cdot \frac{1}{3}$ = 2/15
4. $\frac{16}{5} \cdot \frac{25}{27}$ = 2 26/27
5. $\frac{8}{21} \cdot 2\frac{7}{16}$ = 13/14
6. $1\frac{5}{7} \cdot 2\frac{1}{4}$ = 3 6/7
7. $5\frac{7}{8} \cdot 4$ = 23 1/2
8. $\frac{5}{7} \cdot \frac{7}{5}$ = 1
9. $3\frac{2}{3} \cdot \frac{17}{22}$ = 2 5/6

10. $\frac{5}{6} \cdot 2$ = 1 2/3
11. $8\frac{1}{3} \cdot \frac{3}{4}$ = 6 1/4
12. $4\frac{1}{4} \cdot 3\frac{1}{5}$ = 13 3/5
13. $2\frac{1}{6} \cdot \frac{18}{20}$ = 1 19/20
14. $\frac{21}{35} \cdot 3\frac{4}{7}$ = 2 1/7
15. $1\frac{3}{5} \cdot 2\frac{3}{16}$ = 3 1/2
16. $6\frac{3}{4} \cdot 1\frac{5}{9}$ = 10 1/2
17. $3\frac{1}{3} \cdot 1\frac{3}{18}$ = 3 8/9
18. $\frac{1}{2} \cdot \frac{6}{11} \cdot \frac{3}{5}$ = 9/55

Page 8

# Answer Key

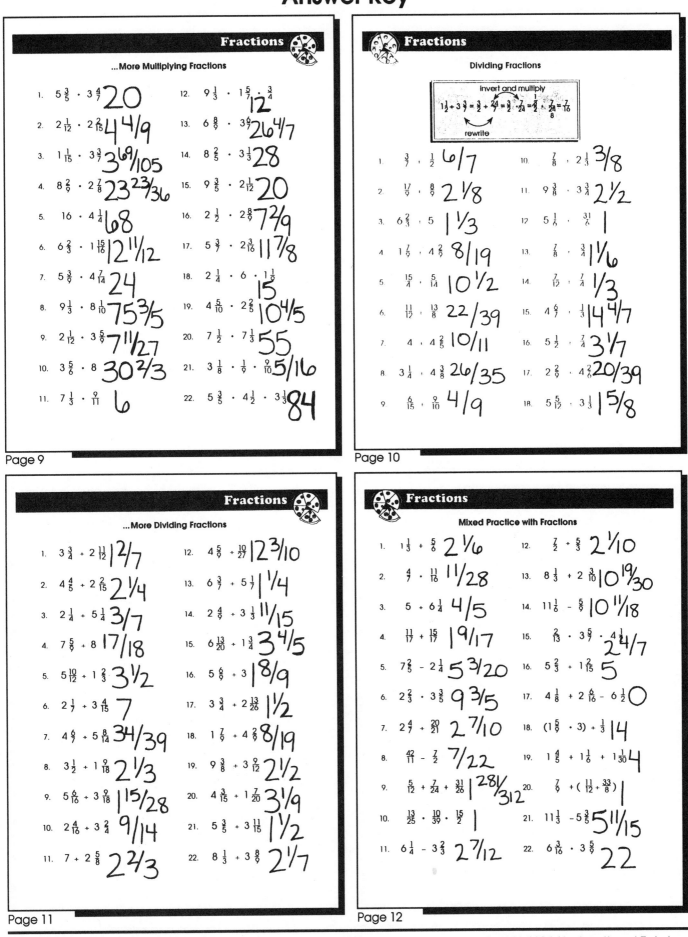

## Fractions

### ...More Multiplying Fractions

1. $5\frac{3}{5} \cdot 3\frac{4}{7}$   20
2. $2\frac{1}{12} \cdot 2\frac{2}{15}$   4 4/9
3. $1\frac{1}{15} \cdot 3\frac{3}{7}$   3 69/105
4. $8\frac{2}{9} \cdot 2\frac{7}{8}$   23 23/36
5. $16 \cdot 4\frac{1}{4}$   68
6. $6\frac{2}{3} \cdot 1\frac{15}{16}$   12 11/12
7. $5\frac{3}{9} \cdot 4\frac{7}{14}$   24
8. $9\frac{1}{3} \cdot 8\frac{1}{10}$   75 3/5
9. $2\frac{1}{12} \cdot 3\frac{5}{9}$   7 11/27
10. $3\frac{5}{6} \cdot 8$   30 2/3
11. $7\frac{1}{3} \cdot \frac{9}{11}$   6

12. $9\frac{1}{3} \cdot 1\frac{5}{7} \cdot \frac{3}{4}$   12
13. $6\frac{8}{9} \cdot 3\frac{6}{7}$   26 4/7
14. $8\frac{2}{5} \cdot 3\frac{1}{3}$   28
15. $9\frac{3}{5} \cdot 2\frac{1}{12}$   20
16. $2\frac{1}{2} \cdot 2\frac{8}{9}$   7 2/9
17. $5\frac{3}{7} \cdot 2\frac{3}{16}$   11 7/8
18. $2\frac{1}{4} \cdot 6 \cdot 1\frac{1}{9}$   15
19. $4\frac{5}{10} \cdot 2\frac{2}{5}$   10 4/5
20. $7\frac{1}{2} \cdot 7\frac{1}{3}$   55
21. $3\frac{1}{8} \cdot \frac{1}{9} \cdot \frac{9}{10}$   5/16
22. $5\frac{3}{5} \cdot 4\frac{1}{2} \cdot 3\frac{1}{3}$   84

**Page 9**

## Fractions

### Dividing Fractions

invert and multiply
$1\frac{1}{2} \div 3\frac{3}{4} = \frac{3}{2} \div \frac{24}{... } = \frac{3}{2} \cdot \frac{1}{24} = \frac{3}{2} \cdot \frac{7}{24} = \frac{7}{16}$
rewrite

1. $\frac{3}{7} \div \frac{1}{2}$   6/7
2. $\frac{17}{9} \div \frac{8}{9}$   2 1/8
3. $6\frac{2}{3} \div 5$   1 1/3
4. $1\frac{7}{9} \div 4\frac{2}{9}$   8/19
5. $\frac{15}{4} \div 5\frac{1}{14}$   10 1/2
6. $\frac{11}{12} \div \frac{13}{8}$   22/39
7. $4 \div 4\frac{2}{5}$   10/11
8. $3\frac{1}{4} \div 4\frac{3}{8}$   26/35
9. $\frac{6}{15} \div \frac{9}{10}$   4/9

10. $\frac{7}{8} \div 2\frac{1}{3}$   3/8
11. $9\frac{3}{8} \div 3\frac{3}{4}$   2 1/2
12. $5\frac{1}{6} \div \frac{31}{6}$   1
13. $\frac{7}{8} \div \frac{3}{4}$   1 1/6
14. $\frac{7}{12} \div \frac{7}{4}$   1/3
15. $4\frac{6}{7} \div \frac{1}{3}$   14 4/7
16. $5\frac{1}{2} \div \frac{7}{4}$   3 1/7
17. $2\frac{2}{9} \div 4\frac{2}{6}$   20/39
18. $5\frac{5}{12} \div 3\frac{1}{3}$   1 5/8

**Page 10**

## Fractions

### ...More Dividing Fractions

1. $3\frac{3}{4} \div 2\frac{11}{12}$   1 2/7
2. $4\frac{4}{5} \div 2\frac{2}{15}$   2 1/4
3. $2\frac{1}{4} \div 5\frac{1}{4}$   3/7
4. $7\frac{5}{9} \div 8$   17/18
5. $5\frac{10}{12} \div 1\frac{2}{3}$   3 1/2
6. $2\frac{1}{7} \div 3\frac{4}{15}$   7
7. $4\frac{6}{7} \div 5\frac{8}{14}$   34/39
8. $3\frac{1}{2} \div 1\frac{9}{18}$   2 1/3
9. $5\frac{6}{16} \div 3\frac{9}{18}$   1 15/28
10. $2\frac{4}{16} \div 3\frac{2}{4}$   9/14
11. $7 \div 2\frac{5}{8}$   2 2/3

12. $4\frac{5}{9} \div \frac{10}{27}$   12 3/10
13. $6\frac{3}{7} \div 5\frac{1}{7}$   1 1/4
14. $2\frac{4}{9} \div 3\frac{1}{3}$   11/15
15. $6\frac{13}{20} \div 1\frac{3}{4}$   3 4/5
16. $5\frac{6}{9} \div 3$   1 8/9
17. $3\frac{3}{4} \div 2\frac{13}{26}$   1 1/2
18. $1\frac{7}{9} \div 4\frac{2}{9}$   8/19
19. $9\frac{3}{8} \div 3\frac{9}{12}$   2 1/2
20. $4\frac{3}{15} \div 1\frac{2}{20}$   3 1/9
21. $5\frac{3}{5} \div 3\frac{11}{15}$   1 1/2
22. $8\frac{1}{3} \div 3\frac{8}{9}$   2 1/7

**Page 11**

## Fractions

### Mixed Practice with Fractions

1. $1\frac{1}{3} + \frac{5}{6}$   2 1/6
2. $\frac{4}{7} \cdot \frac{11}{16}$   11/28
3. $5 \div 6\frac{1}{4}$   4/5
4. $\frac{11}{17} + \frac{15}{17}$   1 9/17
5. $7\frac{2}{5} - 2\frac{1}{4}$   5 3/20
6. $2\frac{2}{3} \cdot 3\frac{3}{5}$   9 3/5
7. $2\frac{4}{7} + \frac{20}{21}$   2 7/10
8. $\frac{42}{11} - \frac{7}{2}$   7/22
9. $\frac{5}{12} + \frac{7}{24} + \frac{31}{26}$   1 281/312
10. $\frac{13}{25} \cdot \frac{10}{39} \cdot \frac{15}{2}$   1
11. $6\frac{1}{4} - 3\frac{2}{3}$   2 7/12

12. $\frac{7}{2} \div \frac{5}{3}$   2 1/10
13. $8\frac{1}{3} + 2\frac{3}{10}$   10 19/30
14. $11\frac{1}{6} - \frac{5}{9}$   10 11/18
15. $\frac{2}{13} \cdot 3\frac{5}{7} \cdot 4\frac{1}{1}$   2 4/7
16. $5\frac{2}{3} + 1\frac{2}{15}$   5
17. $4\frac{1}{8} + 2\frac{6}{16} - 6\frac{1}{2}$   0
18. $(1\frac{5}{9} \cdot 3) \div \frac{1}{3}$   14
19. $1\frac{4}{5} + 1\frac{1}{6} + 1\frac{1}{30}$   4
20. $\frac{7}{9} \div (\frac{11}{12} + \frac{33}{8})$   1
21. $11\frac{1}{3} - 5\frac{3}{5}$   5 11/15
22. $6\frac{3}{16} \cdot 3\frac{5}{9}$   22

**Page 12**

# Answer Key

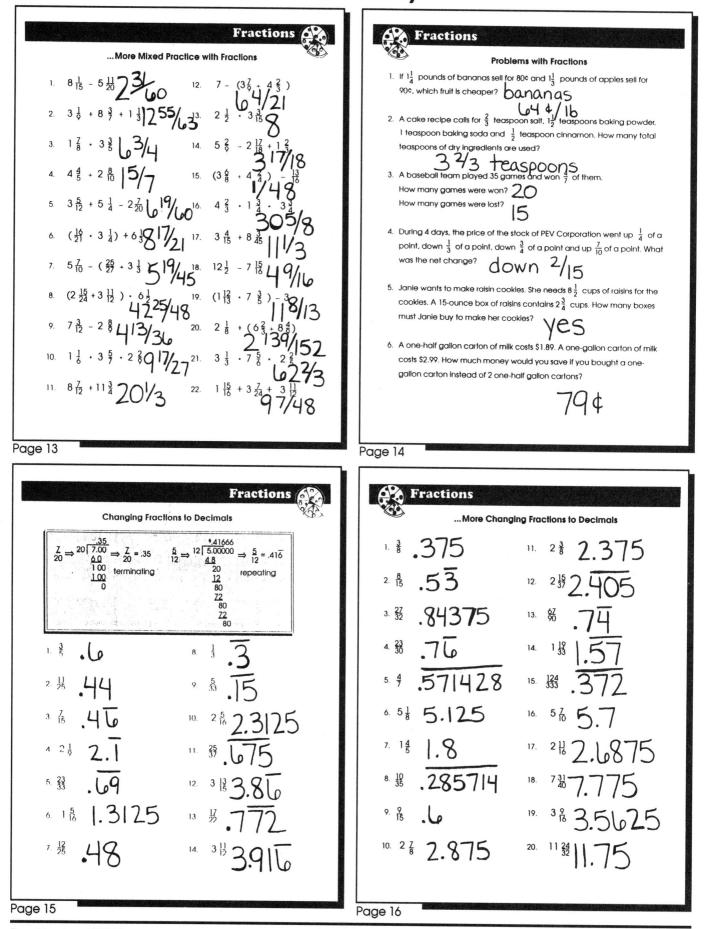

## Fractions — ...More Mixed Practice with Fractions (Page 13)

1. $8\frac{1}{15} - 5\frac{11}{20}$  = $2\frac{31}{60}$
2. $3\frac{1}{9} + 8\frac{3}{7} + 1\frac{1}{3}$  = $12\frac{55}{63}$
3. $1\frac{7}{8} \cdot 3\frac{3}{5}$  = $6\frac{3}{4}$
4. $4\frac{4}{5} + 2\frac{8}{10}$  = $1\frac{5}{7}$
5. $3\frac{5}{12} + 5\frac{1}{4} - 2\frac{7}{20}$  = $6\frac{19}{60}$
6. $(\frac{16}{21} \cdot 3\frac{1}{4}) + 6\frac{1}{3}$  = $8\frac{17}{21}$
7. $5\frac{7}{10} - (\frac{25}{27} + 3\frac{1}{3})$  = $1\frac{19}{45}$
8. $(2\frac{15}{24} + 3\frac{11}{12}) \cdot 6\frac{1}{2}$  = $42\frac{25}{48}$
9. $7\frac{3}{12} - 2\frac{8}{9}$  = $4\frac{13}{36}$
10. $1\frac{1}{6} \cdot 3\frac{5}{7} \cdot 2\frac{2}{9}$  = $9\frac{17}{27}$
11. $8\frac{7}{12} + 11\frac{3}{4}$  = $20\frac{1}{3}$

12. $7 - (3\frac{7}{9} + 4\frac{2}{7})$  = $-1\frac{4}{21}$
13. $2\frac{1}{2} \cdot 3\frac{1}{5}$  = $8$
14. $5\frac{2}{9} - 2\frac{17}{18} + 1\frac{2}{3}$  = $3\frac{17}{18}$
15. $(3\frac{6}{8} + 4\frac{2}{4}) - \frac{13}{16}$  = $\frac{1}{48}$
16. $4\frac{2}{3} \cdot 1\frac{3}{4} \cdot 3\frac{3}{4}$  = $30\frac{5}{8}$
17. $3\frac{4}{15} + 8\frac{3}{45}$  = $11\frac{1}{3}$
18. $12\frac{1}{2} - 7\frac{15}{16}$  = $4\frac{9}{16}$
19. $(1\frac{12}{13} \cdot 7\frac{3}{5}) - 3$  = $11\frac{8}{13}$
20. $2\frac{1}{8} + (6\frac{2}{3} + 8\frac{4}{5})$  = $2\frac{139}{152}$
21. $3\frac{1}{3} \cdot 7\frac{5}{8} \cdot 2\frac{4}{5}$  = $62\frac{2}{3}$
22. $1\frac{15}{16} + 3\frac{7}{24} + 3\frac{11}{12}$  = $9\frac{7}{48}$

## Fractions — Problems with Fractions (Page 14)

1. If $1\frac{1}{4}$ pounds of bananas sell for 80¢ and $1\frac{1}{3}$ pounds of apples sell for 90¢, which fruit is cheaper?  **bananas  64 ¢/lb**
2. A cake recipe calls for $\frac{2}{3}$ teaspoon salt, $1\frac{1}{2}$ teaspoons baking powder, 1 teaspoon baking soda and $\frac{1}{2}$ teaspoon cinnamon. How many total teaspoons of dry ingredients are used?  **$3\frac{2}{3}$ teaspoons**
3. A baseball team played 35 games and won $\frac{4}{7}$ of them. How many games were won? **20** How many games were lost? **15**
4. During 4 days, the price of the stock of PEV Corporation went up $\frac{1}{4}$ of a point, down $\frac{1}{3}$ of a point, down $\frac{3}{4}$ of a point and up $\frac{7}{10}$ of a point. What was the net change?  **down $\frac{2}{15}$**
5. Janie wants to make raisin cookies. She needs $8\frac{1}{2}$ cups of raisins for the cookies. A 15-ounce box of raisins contains $2\frac{3}{4}$ cups. How many boxes must Janie buy to make her cookies?  **yes**
6. A one-half gallon carton of milk costs $1.89. A one-gallon carton of milk costs $2.99. How much money would you save if you bought a one-gallon carton instead of 2 one-half gallon cartons?  **79¢**

## Fractions — Changing Fractions to Decimals (Page 15)

$\frac{7}{20} \Rightarrow 20\overline{)7.00} \Rightarrow \frac{7}{20} = .35$  terminating

$\frac{5}{12} \Rightarrow 12\overline{)5.00000} \Rightarrow \frac{5}{12} = .41\overline{6}$  repeating

1. $\frac{3}{5}$  = .6
2. $\frac{11}{25}$  = .44
3. $\frac{7}{15}$  = .4$\overline{6}$
4. $2\frac{1}{9}$  = 2.$\overline{1}$
5. $\frac{23}{33}$  = .$\overline{69}$
6. $1\frac{5}{16}$  = 1.3125
7. $\frac{12}{25}$  = .48
8. $\frac{1}{3}$  = .$\overline{3}$
9. $\frac{5}{33}$  = .$\overline{15}$
10. $2\frac{5}{16}$  = 2.3125
11. $\frac{25}{37}$  = .$\overline{675}$
12. $3\frac{13}{15}$  = 3.8$\overline{6}$
13. $\frac{17}{22}$  = .7$\overline{72}$
14. $3\frac{11}{12}$  = 3.91$\overline{6}$

## Fractions — ...More Changing Fractions to Decimals (Page 16)

1. $\frac{3}{8}$  = .375
2. $\frac{8}{15}$  = .5$\overline{3}$
3. $\frac{27}{32}$  = .84375
4. $\frac{23}{30}$  = .7$\overline{6}$
5. $\frac{4}{7}$  = .$\overline{571428}$
6. $5\frac{1}{8}$  = 5.125
7. $1\frac{4}{5}$  = 1.8
8. $\frac{10}{35}$  = .$\overline{285714}$
9. $\frac{9}{15}$  = .6
10. $2\frac{7}{8}$  = 2.875
11. $2\frac{3}{8}$  = 2.375
12. $2\frac{15}{37}$  = 2.$\overline{405}$
13. $\frac{67}{90}$  = .7$\overline{4}$
14. $1\frac{19}{33}$  = 1.$\overline{57}$
15. $\frac{124}{333}$  = .$\overline{372}$
16. $5\frac{7}{10}$  = 5.7
17. $2\frac{11}{16}$  = 2.6875
18. $7\frac{31}{40}$  = 7.775
19. $3\frac{9}{18}$  = 3.5625
20. $11\frac{24}{32}$  = 11.75

# Answer Key

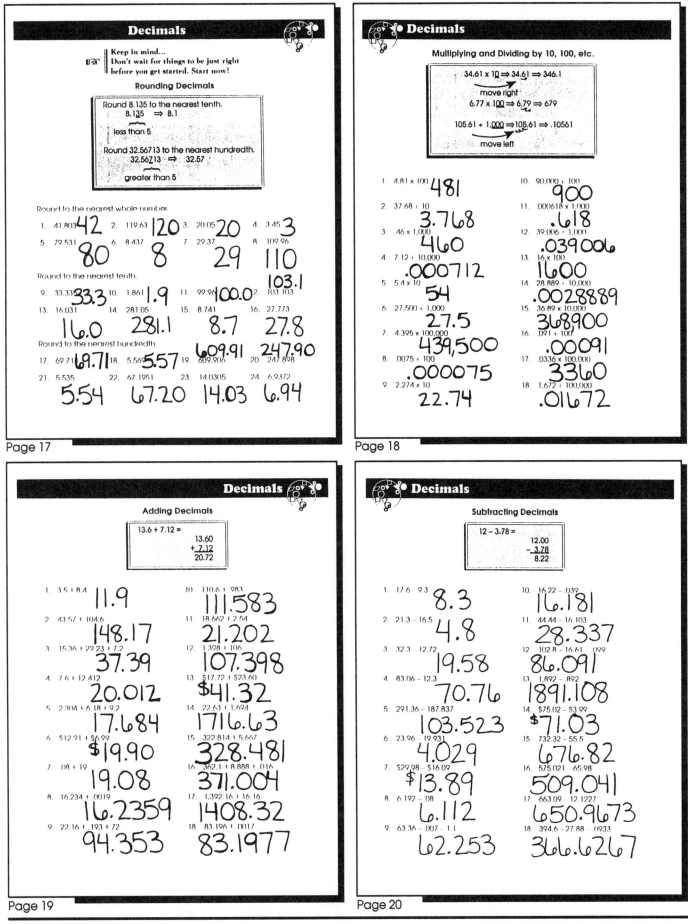

## Decimals

☞ **Keep in mind...**
Don't wait for things to be just right before you get started. Start now!

### Rounding Decimals

Round 8.135 to the nearest tenth.
8.135 ⟹ 8.1

less than 5

Round 32.56713 to the nearest hundredth.
32.56713 ⟹ 32.57

greater than 5

Round to the nearest whole number.

1. 41.803 **42**   2. 119.63 **120**   3. 20.05 **20**   4. 3.45 **3**
5. 79.531 **80**   6. 8.437 **8**   7. 29.37 **29**   8. 109.96 **110**

Round to the nearest tenth.

9. 33.33 **33.3**   10. 1.861 **1.9**   11. 99.96 **100.0**   12. 103.103 **103.1**
13. 16.031 **16.0**   14. 281.05 **281.1**   15. 8.741 **8.7**   16. 27.773 **27.8**

Round to the nearest hundredth.

17. 69.71 **69.71**   18. 5.569 **5.57**   19. 609.906 **609.91**   20. 247.898 **247.90**
21. 5.535 **5.54**   22. 67.1951 **67.20**   23. 14.0305 **14.03**   24. 6.9372 **6.94**

## Decimals

### Multiplying and Dividing by 10, 100, etc.

34.61 x 10 ⟹ 34.61 ⟹ 346.1
move right
6.77 x 100 ⟹ 6.79 ⟹ 679
105.61 ÷ 1,000 ⟹ 105.61 ⟹ .10561
move left

1. 4.81 x 100 **481**
2. 37.68 ÷ 10 **3.768**
3. .46 x 1,000 **460**
4. 7.12 ÷ 10,000 **.000712**
5. 5.4 x 10 **54**
6. 27,500 ÷ 1,000 **27.5**
7. 4.395 x 100,000 **439,500**
8. .0075 ÷ 100 **.000075**
9. 2.274 x 10 **22.74**
10. 90,000 ÷ 100 **900**
11. .000618 x 1,000 **.618**
12. 39.006 ÷ 1,000 **.039006**
13. 16 x 100 **1600**
14. 28.889 ÷ 10,000 **.0028889**
15. 36.89 x 10,000 **368900**
16. .091 ÷ 100 **.00091**
17. .0336 x 100,000 **3360**
18. 1.672 ÷ 100,000 **.01672**

## Decimals

### Adding Decimals

13.6 + 7.12 =
13.60
+ 7.12
20.72

1. 3.5 + 8.4 **11.9**
2. 43.57 + 104.6 **148.17**
3. 15.36 + 29.23 + 7.2 **37.39**
4. 7.6 + 12.412 **20.012**
5. 2.304 + 6.18 + 9.2 **17.684**
6. $12.91 + $6.99 **$19.90**
7. .08 + 19 **19.08**
8. 16.234 + .0019 **16.2359**
9. 22.16 + .193 + 72 **94.353**
10. 110.6 + 98.3 **111.583**
11. 18.662 + 2.54 **21.202**
12. 1.398 + 106 **107.398**
13. $17.72 + $23.60 **$41.32**
14. 22.63 + 1.694 **1716.63**
15. 322.814 + 5.667 **328.481**
16. 362.1 + 8.888 + .016 **371.004**
17. 1,392.16 + 16.16 **1408.32**
18. 83.196 + .0017 **83.1977**

## Decimals

### Subtracting Decimals

12 – 3.78 =
12.00
– 3.78
8.22

1. 17.6 – 9.3 **8.3**
2. 21.3 – 16.5 **4.8**
3. 32.3 – 12.72 **19.58**
4. 83.06 – 12.3 **70.76**
5. 291.36 – 187.837 **103.523**
6. 23.96 – 19.931 **4.029**
7. $29.98 – $16.09 **$13.89**
8. 6.192 – .08 **6.112**
9. 63.36 – .007 – 1.1 **62.253**
10. 16.22 – .039 **16.181**
11. 44.44 – 16.103 **28.337**
12. 102.8 – 16.61 – .099 **86.091**
13. 1,892 – .892 **1891.108**
14. $75.02 – $3.99 **$71.03**
15. 732.32 – 55.5 **676.82**
16. 575.021 – 65.98 **509.041**
17. 663.09 – 12.1227 **650.9673**
18. 394.6 – 27.88 – .0933 **366.6267**

# Answer Key

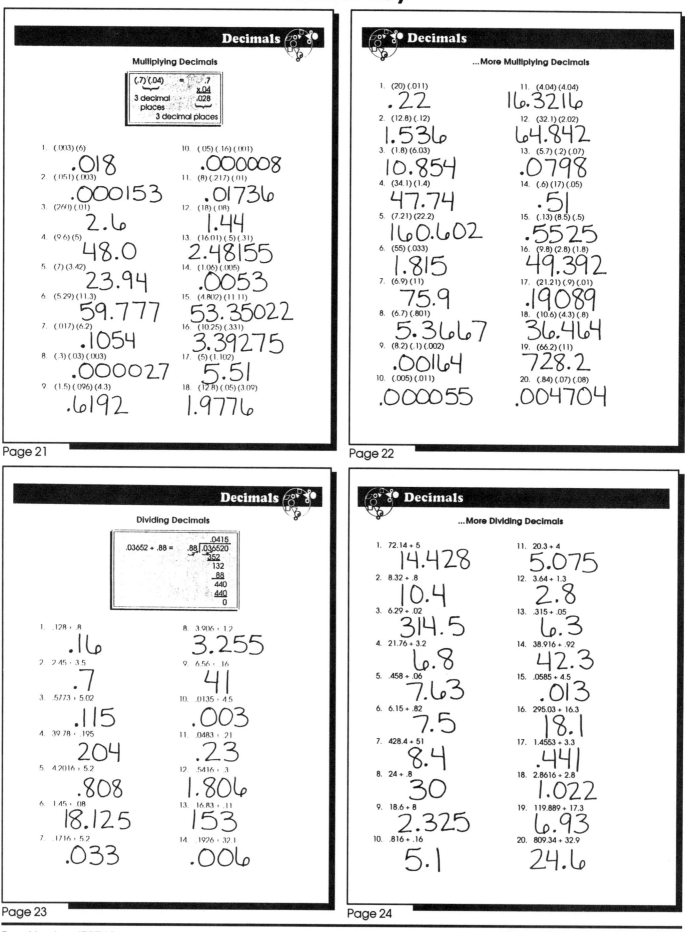

## Decimals

### Multiplying Decimals

$(.7)(.04) =$
$\begin{array}{r} .7 \\ \times .04 \\ \hline .028 \end{array}$

3 decimal places
3 decimal places

1. (.003) (6)
.018

2. (.051) (.003)
.000153

3. (260) (.01)
2.6

4. (9.6) (5)
48.0

5. (7) (3.42)
23.94

6. (5.29) (11.3)
59.777

7. (.017) (6.2)
.1054

8. (.3) (.03) (.003)
.000027

9. (1.5) (.096) (4.3)
.6192

10. (.05) (.16) (.001)
.000008

11. (8) (.217) (.01)
.01736

12. (18) (.08)
1.44

13. (16.01) (.5) (.31)
2.48155

14. (1.06) (.005)
.0053

15. (4.802) (11.11)
53.35022

16. (10.25) (.331)
3.39275

17. (5) (1.102)
5.51

18. (12.8) (.05) (3.09)
1.9776

Page 21

## Decimals

### ...More Multiplying Decimals

1. (20) (.011)
.22

2. (12.8) (.12)
1.536

3. (1.8) (6.03)
10.854

4. (34.1) (1.4)
47.74

5. (7.21) (22.2)
160.602

6. (55) (.033)
1.815

7. (6.9) (11)
75.9

8. (6.7) (.801)
5.3667

9. (8.2) (.1) (.002)
.00164

10. (.005) (.011)
.000055

11. (4.04) (4.04)
16.3216

12. (32.1) (2.02)
64.842

13. (5.7) (.2) (.07)
.0798

14. (.6) (17) (.05)
.51

15. (.13) (8.5) (.5)
.5525

16. (9.8) (2.8) (1.8)
49.392

17. (21.21) (.9) (.01)
.19089

18. (10.6) (4.3) (.8)
36.464

19. (66.2) (11)
728.2

20. (.84) (.07) (.08)
.004704

Page 22

## Decimals

### Dividing Decimals

$.03652 \div .88 =$
$\begin{array}{r} .0415 \\ .88\overline{)\,.036520} \\ \underline{352} \\ 132 \\ \underline{88} \\ 440 \\ \underline{440} \\ 0 \end{array}$

1. .128 ÷ .8
.16

2. 2.45 ÷ 3.5
.7

3. .5773 ÷ 5.02
.115

4. 39.78 ÷ .195
204

5. 4.2016 ÷ 5.2
.808

6. 1.45 ÷ .08
18.125

7. .1716 ÷ 5.2
.033

8. 3.906 ÷ 1.2
3.255

9. 6.56 ÷ .16
41

10. .0135 ÷ 4.5
.003

11. .0483 ÷ .21
.23

12. .5416 ÷ .3
1.806

13. 16.83 ÷ .11
153

14. .1926 ÷ 32.1
.006

Page 23

## Decimals

### ...More Dividing Decimals

1. 72.14 ÷ 5
14.428

2. 8.32 ÷ .8
10.4

3. 6.29 ÷ .02
314.5

4. 21.76 ÷ 3.2
6.8

5. .458 ÷ .06
7.63

6. 6.15 ÷ .82
7.5

7. 428.4 ÷ 51
8.4

8. 24 ÷ .8
30

9. 18.6 ÷ 8
2.325

10. .816 ÷ .16
5.1

11. 20.3 ÷ 4
5.075

12. 3.64 ÷ 1.3
2.8

13. .315 ÷ .05
6.3

14. 38.916 ÷ .92
42.3

15. .0585 ÷ 4.5
.013

16. 295.03 ÷ 16.3
18.1

17. 1.4553 ÷ 3.3
.441

18. 2.8616 ÷ 2.8
1.022

19. 119.889 ÷ 17.3
6.93

20. 809.34 ÷ 32.9
24.6

Page 24

# Answer Key

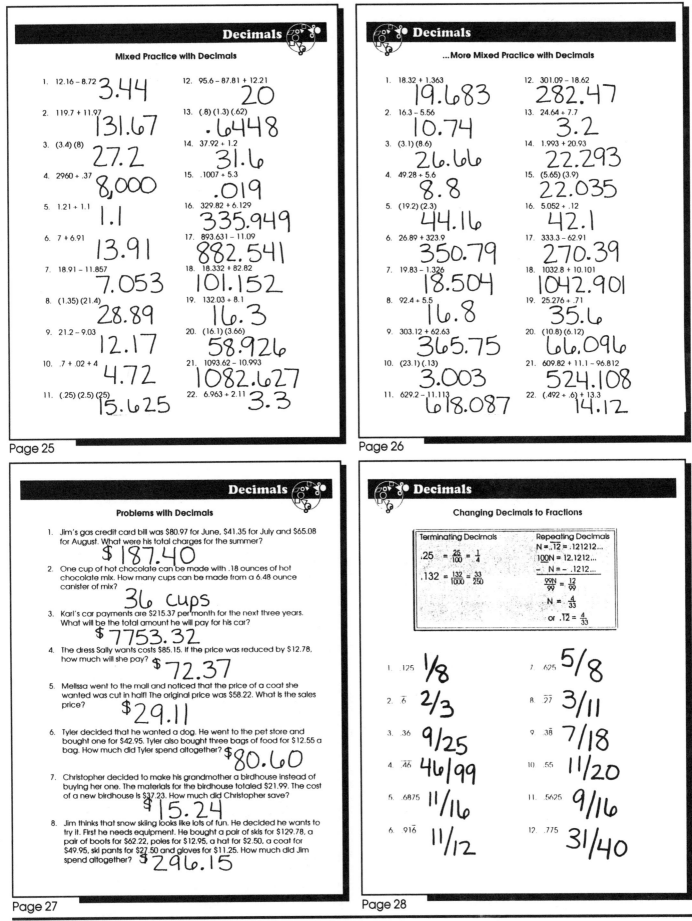

## Decimals
### Mixed Practice with Decimals

1. 12.16 – 8.72    3.44
2. 119.7 + 11.97    131.67
3. (3.4) (8)    27.2
4. 2960 ÷ .37    8,000
5. 1.21 ÷ 1.1    1.1
6. 7 + 6.91    13.91
7. 18.91 – 11.857    7.053
8. (1.35) (21.4)    28.89
9. 21.2 – 9.03    12.17
10. .7 + .02 + 4    4.72
11. (.25) (2.5) (25)    15.625
12. 95.6 – 87.81 + 12.21    20
13. (.8) (1.3) (.62)    .6448
14. 37.92 ÷ 1.2    31.6
15. .1007 ÷ 5.3    .019
16. 329.82 + 6.129    335.949
17. 893.631 – 11.09    882.541
18. 18.332 + 82.82    101.152
19. 132.03 ÷ 8.1    16.3
20. (16.1) (3.66)    58.926
21. 1093.62 – 10.993    1082.627
22. 6.963 + 2.11    3.3

**Page 25**

## Decimals
### ...More Mixed Practice with Decimals

1. 18.32 + 1.363    19.683
2. 16.3 – 5.56    10.74
3. (3.1) (8.6)    26.66
4. 49.28 ÷ 5.6    8.8
5. (19.2) (2.3)    44.16
6. 26.89 + 323.9    350.79
7. 19.83 – 1.326    18.504
8. 92.4 ÷ 5.5    16.8
9. 303.12 + 62.63    365.75
10. (23.1) (.13)    3.003
11. 629.2 – 11.113    618.087
12. 301.09 – 18.62    282.47
13. 24.64 ÷ 7.7    3.2
14. 1.993 + 20.93    22.293
15. (5.65) (3.9)    22.035
16. 5.052 ÷ .12    42.1
17. 333.3 – 62.91    270.39
18. 1032.8 + 10.101    1042.901
19. 25.276 ÷ .71    35.6
20. (10.8) (6.12)    66.096
21. 609.82 + 11.1 – 96.812    524.108
22. (.492 + .6) + 13.3    14.12

**Page 26**

## Decimals
### Problems with Decimals

1. Jim's gas credit card bill was $80.97 for June, $41.35 for July and $65.08 for August. What were his total charges for the summer?
   $187.40
2. One cup of hot chocolate can be made with .18 ounces of hot chocolate mix. How many cups can be made from a 6.48 ounce canister of mix?
   36 cups
3. Karl's car payments are $215.37 per month for the next three years. What will be the total amount he will pay for his car?
   $7753.32
4. The dress Sally wants costs $85.15. If the price was reduced by $12.78, how much will she pay?    $72.37
5. Melissa went to the mall and noticed that the price of a coat she wanted was cut in half! The original price was $58.22. What is the sales price?
   $29.11
6. Tyler decided that he wanted a dog. He went to the pet store and bought one for $42.95. Tyler also bought three bags of food for $12.55 a bag. How much did Tyler spend altogether?    $80.60
7. Christopher decided to make his grandmother a birdhouse instead of buying her one. The materials for the birdhouse totaled $21.99. The cost of a new birdhouse is $37.23. How much did Christopher save?
   $15.24
8. Jim thinks that snow skiing looks like lots of fun. He decided he wants to try it. First he needs equipment. He bought a pair of skis for $129.78, a pair of boots for $62.22, poles for $12.95, a hat for $2.50, a coat for $49.95, ski pants for $27.50 and gloves for $11.25. How much did Jim spend altogether?    $296.15

**Page 27**

## Decimals
### Changing Decimals to Fractions

| Terminating Decimals | Repeating Decimals |
|---|---|
| $.25 = \frac{25}{100} = \frac{1}{4}$ | $N = .\overline{12} = .121212...$ |
| | $100N = 12.1212...$ |
| $.132 = \frac{132}{1000} = \frac{33}{250}$ | $-\ N = -\ .1212...$ |
| | $\frac{99N}{99} = \frac{12}{99}$ |
| | $N = \frac{4}{33}$ |
| | or $.\overline{12} = \frac{4}{33}$ |

1. .125    1/8
2. .$\overline{6}$    2/3
3. .36    9/25
4. .$\overline{46}$    46/99
5. .6875    11/16
6. .91$\overline{6}$    11/12
7. .625    5/8
8. .$\overline{27}$    3/11
9. .38$\overline{8}$    7/18
10. .55    11/20
11. .5625    9/16
12. .775    31/40

**Page 28**

# Answer Key

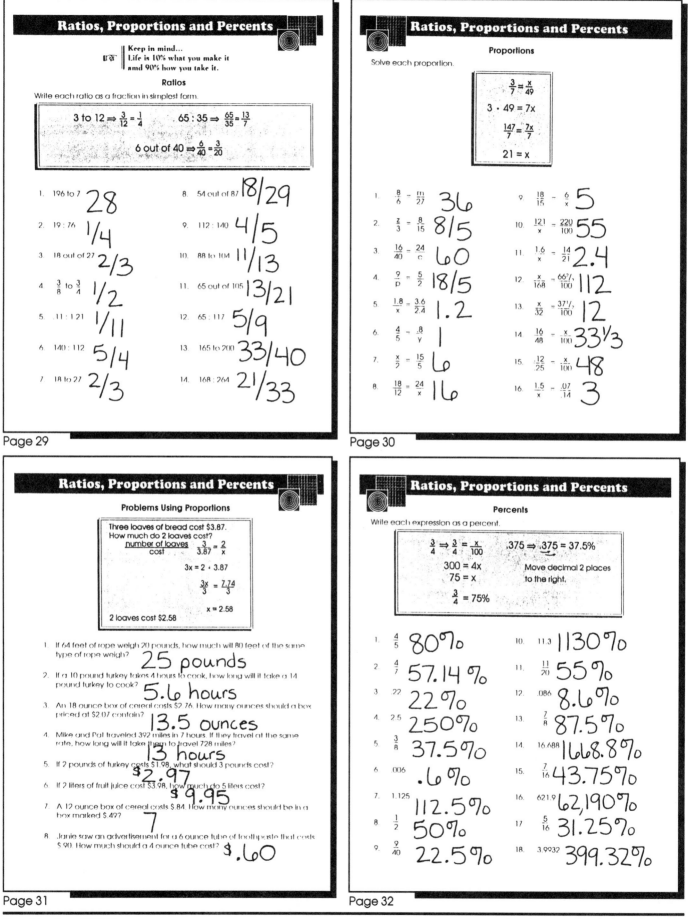

## Ratios, Proportions and Percents

☞ Keep in mind...
Life is 10% what you make it
and 90% how you take it.

### Ratios

Write each ratio as a fraction in simplest form.

$$3 \text{ to } 12 \Rightarrow \frac{3}{12} = \frac{1}{4} \qquad 65 : 35 \Rightarrow \frac{65}{35} = \frac{13}{7}$$

$$6 \text{ out of } 40 \Rightarrow \frac{6}{40} = \frac{3}{20}$$

1. 196 to 7 — **28**
2. 19 : 76 — **1/4**
3. 18 out of 27 — **2/3**
4. $\frac{3}{8}$ to $\frac{3}{4}$ — **1/2**
5. 11 : 121 — **1/11**
6. 140 : 112 — **5/4**
7. 18 to 27 — **2/3**
8. 54 out of 87 — **18/29**
9. 112 : 140 — **4/5**
10. 88 to 104 — **11/13**
11. 65 out of 105 — **13/21**
12. 65 : 117 — **5/9**
13. 165 to 200 — **33/40**
14. 168 : 264 — **21/33**

Page 29

## Ratios, Proportions and Percents

### Proportions

Solve each proportion.

$$\frac{3}{7} = \frac{x}{49}$$
$$3 \cdot 49 = 7x$$
$$\frac{147}{7} = \frac{7x}{7}$$
$$21 = x$$

1. $\frac{8}{6} = \frac{m}{27}$ — **36**
2. $\frac{z}{3} = \frac{8}{15}$ — **8/5**
3. $\frac{16}{40} = \frac{24}{c}$ — **60**
4. $\frac{9}{p} = \frac{5}{2}$ — **18/5**
5. $\frac{1.8}{x} = \frac{3.6}{2.4}$ — **1.2**
6. $\frac{4}{5} = \frac{.8}{y}$ — **1**
7. $\frac{x}{2} = \frac{15}{5}$ — **6**
8. $\frac{18}{12} = \frac{24}{x}$ — **16**
9. $\frac{18}{15} = \frac{6}{x}$ — **5**
10. $\frac{121}{x} = \frac{220}{100}$ — **55**
11. $\frac{1.6}{x} = \frac{14}{21}$ — **2.4**
12. $\frac{x}{168} = \frac{66\frac{2}{3}}{100}$ — **112**
13. $\frac{x}{32} = \frac{37\frac{1}{2}}{100}$ — **12**
14. $\frac{16}{48} = \frac{x}{100}$ — **33⅓**
15. $\frac{.12}{.25} = \frac{x}{100}$ — **48**
16. $\frac{1.5}{x} = \frac{.07}{.14}$ — **3**

Page 30

## Ratios, Proportions and Percents

### Problems Using Proportions

Three loaves of bread cost $3.87.
How much do 2 loaves cost?
$$\frac{\text{number of loaves}}{\text{cost}} \qquad \frac{3}{3.87} = \frac{2}{x}$$
$$3x = 2 \cdot 3.87$$
$$\frac{3x}{3} = \frac{7.74}{3}$$
$$x = 2.58$$
2 loaves cost $2.58

1. If 64 feet of rope weigh 20 pounds, how much will 80 feet of the same type of rope weigh? **25 pounds**
2. If a 10 pound turkey takes 4 hours to cook, how long will it take a 14 pound turkey to cook? **5.6 hours**
3. An 18 ounce box of cereal costs $2.76. How many ounces should a box priced at $2.07 contain? **13.5 ounces**
4. Mike and Pat traveled 392 miles in 7 hours. If they travel at the same rate, how long will it take them to travel 728 miles? **13 hours**
5. If 2 pounds of turkey costs $1.98, what should 3 pounds cost? **$2.97**
6. If 2 liters of fruit juice cost $3.98, how much do 5 liters cost? **$9.95**
7. A 12 ounce box of cereal costs $.84. How many ounces should be in a box marked $.49? **7**
8. Janie saw an advertisement for a 6 ounce tube of toothpaste that costs $.90. How much should a 4 ounce tube cost? **$.60**

Page 31

## Ratios, Proportions and Percents

### Percents

Write each expression as a percent.

$$\frac{3}{4} \Rightarrow \frac{3}{4} = \frac{x}{100} \qquad .375 \Rightarrow .375 = 37.5\%$$
$$300 = 4x \qquad \text{Move decimal 2 places}$$
$$75 = x \qquad \text{to the right.}$$
$$\frac{3}{4} = 75\%$$

1. $\frac{4}{5}$ — **80%**
2. $\frac{4}{7}$ — **57.14%**
3. .22 — **22%**
4. 2.5 — **250%**
5. $\frac{3}{8}$ — **37.5%**
6. .006 — **.6%**
7. 1.125 — **112.5%**
8. $\frac{1}{2}$ — **50%**
9. $\frac{9}{40}$ — **22.5%**
10. 11.3 — **1130%**
11. $\frac{11}{20}$ — **55%**
12. .086 — **8.6%**
13. $\frac{7}{8}$ — **87.5%**
14. 16.688 — **1668.8%**
15. $\frac{7}{16}$ — **43.75%**
16. 621.9 — **62,190%**
17. $\frac{5}{16}$ — **31.25%**
18. 3.9932 — **399.32%**

Page 32

# Answer Key

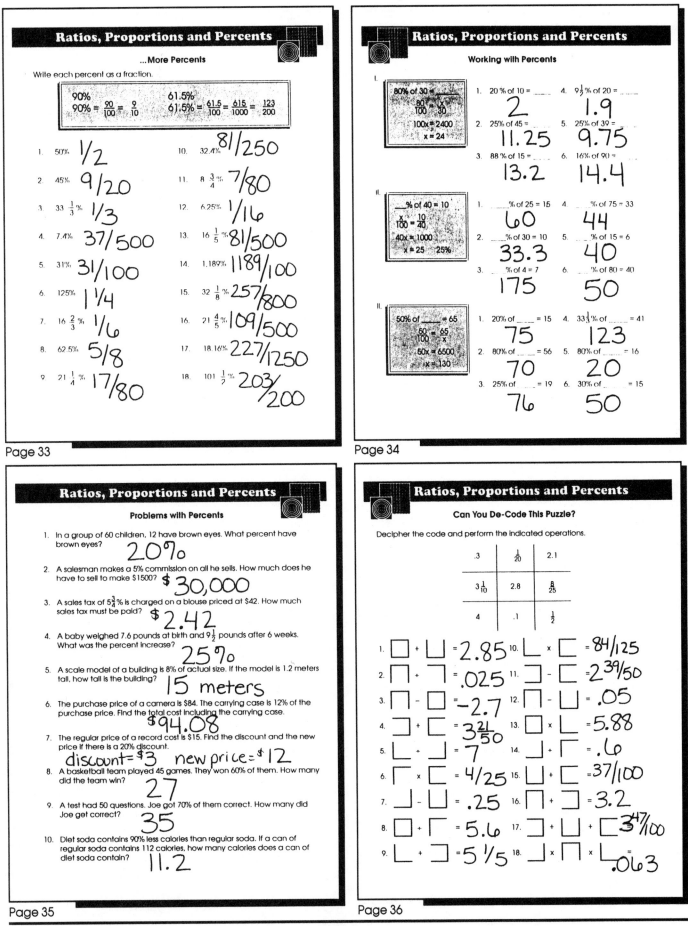

## Ratios, Proportions and Percents
### ...More Percents

Write each percent as a fraction.

| 90% | 61.5% |
|---|---|
| $90\% = \frac{90}{100} = \frac{9}{10}$ | $61.5\% = \frac{61.5}{100} = \frac{615}{1000} = \frac{123}{200}$ |

1. 50%  $\frac{1}{2}$
2. 45%  $\frac{9}{20}$
3. $33\frac{1}{3}\%$  $\frac{1}{3}$
4. 7.4%  $\frac{37}{500}$
5. 31%  $\frac{31}{100}$
6. 125%  $1\frac{1}{4}$
7. $16\frac{2}{3}\%$  $\frac{1}{6}$
8. 62.5%  $\frac{5}{8}$
9. $21\frac{1}{4}\%$  $\frac{17}{80}$

10. 32.4%  $\frac{81}{250}$
11. $8\frac{3}{4}\%$  $\frac{7}{80}$
12. 6.25%  $\frac{1}{16}$
13. $16\frac{1}{5}\%$  $\frac{81}{500}$
14. 1.189%  $\frac{1189}{100}$
15. $32\frac{1}{8}\%$  $\frac{257}{800}$
16. $21\frac{4}{5}\%$  $\frac{109}{500}$
17. 18.16%  $\frac{227}{1250}$
18. $101\frac{1}{2}\%$  $\frac{203}{200}$

Page 33

## Ratios, Proportions and Percents
### Working with Percents

I.
80% of 30 =
$\frac{80}{100} = \frac{x}{30}$
$100x = 2400$
$x = 24$

1. 20% of 10 =  2
2. 25% of 45 =  11.25
3. 88% of 15 =  13.2
4. $9\frac{1}{2}\%$ of 20 =  1.9
5. 25% of 39 =  9.75
6. 16% of 90 =  14.4

II.
___% of 40 = 10
$\frac{x}{100} = \frac{10}{40}$
$40x = 1000$
$x = 25$  25%

1. ___% of 25 = 15  60
2. ___% of 30 = 10  33.3
3. ___% of 4 = 7  175
4. ___% of 75 = 33  44
5. ___% of 15 = 6  40
6. ___% of 80 = 40  50

III.
50% of ___ = 65
$\frac{50}{100} = \frac{65}{x}$
$50x = 6500$
$x = 130$

1. 20% of ___ = 15  75
2. 80% of ___ = 56  70
3. 25% of ___ = 19  76
4. $33\frac{1}{3}\%$ of ___ = 41  123
5. 80% of ___ = 16  20
6. 30% of ___ = 15  50

Page 34

## Ratios, Proportions and Percents
### Problems with Percents

1. In a group of 60 children, 12 have brown eyes. What percent have brown eyes?  20%
2. A salesman makes a 5% commission on all he sells. How much does he have to sell to make $1500?  $30,000
3. A sales tax of $5\frac{3}{4}$% is charged on a blouse priced at $42. How much sales tax must be paid?  $2.42
4. A baby weighed 7.6 pounds at birth and $9\frac{1}{2}$ pounds after 6 weeks. What was the percent increase?  25%
5. A scale model of a building is 8% of actual size. If the model is 1.2 meters tall, how tall is the building?  15 meters
6. The purchase price of a camera is $84. The carrying case is 12% of the purchase price. Find the total cost including the carrying case.  $94.08
7. The regular price of a record cost is $15. Find the discount and the new price if there is a 20% discount.  discount = $3  new price = $12
8. A basketball team played 45 games. They won 60% of them. How many did the team win?  27
9. A test had 50 questions. Joe got 70% of them correct. How many did Joe get correct?  35
10. Diet soda contains 90% less calories than regular soda. If a can of regular soda contains 112 calories, how many calories does a can of diet soda contain?  11.2

Page 35

## Ratios, Proportions and Percents
### Can You De-Code This Puzzle?

Decipher the code and perform the indicated operations.

| .3 | $\frac{1}{20}$ | 2.1 |
|---|---|---|
| $3\frac{1}{10}$ | 2.8 | $\frac{8}{25}$ |
| 4 | .1 | $\frac{1}{2}$ |

1. □ + ⊔ = 2.85
2. ⊓ + ⊐ = .025
3. ⊓ − □ = −2.7
4. □ + ⊏ = $3\frac{21}{50}$
5. ⌐ + ⊔ = 7
6. ⌐ × □ = 4/25
7. ⊔ − ⊔ = .25
8. □ + ⌐ = 5.6
9. ⌐ + ⊐ = $5\frac{1}{5}$
10. ⌐ × □ = 84/125
11. ⊐ − □ = $2\frac{39}{50}$
12. ⊓ − ⊔ = .05
13. □ × ⌐ = 5.88
14. ⊔ + □ = .6
15. ⊔ + ⊏ = 37/100
16. ⊓ + ⊐ = 3.2
17. ⊐ + ⊔ + ⊏ = $3\frac{47}{100}$
18. ⊔ × ⊓ × ⌐ = .063

Page 36

# Answer Key

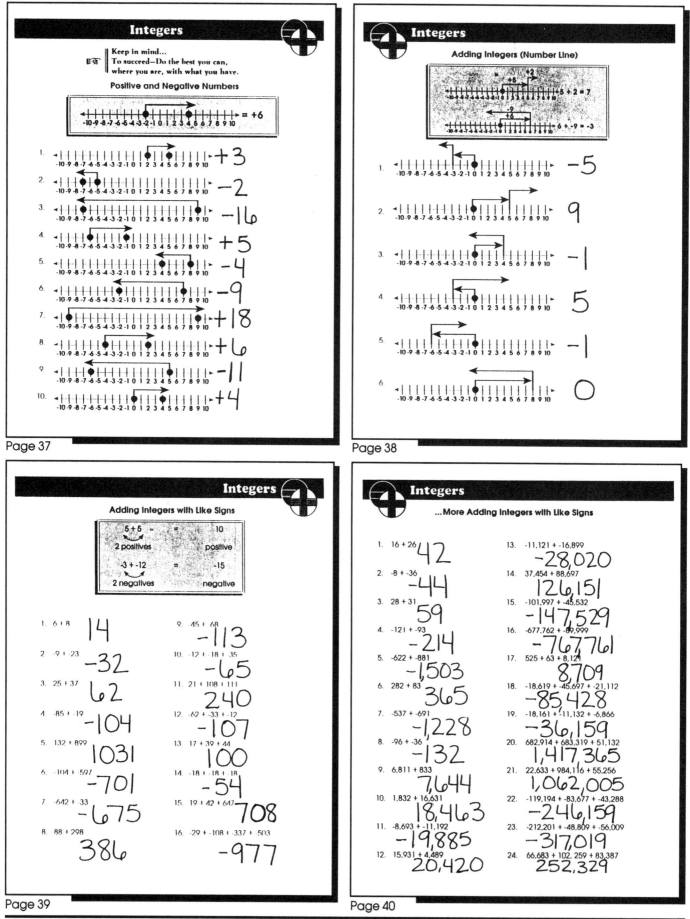

## Integers

**Positive and Negative Numbers**

Keep in mind...
To succeed—Do the best you can, where you are, with what you have.

= +6

1. +3
2. −2
3. −16
4. +5
5. −4
6. −9
7. +18
8. +6
9. −11
10. +4

## Integers

**Adding Integers (Number Line)**

5 + 2 = 7
6 + -9 = -3

1. −5
2. 9
3. −1
4. 5
5. −1
6. 0

## Integers

**Adding Integers with Like Signs**

5 + 5 = 10
2 positives positive
-3 + -12 = -15
2 negatives negative

1. 6 + 8    14
2. -9 + -23    −32
3. 25 + 37    62
4. -85 + -19    −104
5. 132 + 899    1031
6. -104 + -597    −701
7. -642 + -33    −675
8. 88 + 298    386

9. -45 + -68    −113
10. -12 + -18 + -35    −65
11. 21 + 108 + 111    240
12. -62 + -33 + -12    −107
13. 17 + 39 + 44    100
14. -18 + -18 + -18    −54
15. 19 + 42 + 647    708
16. -29 + -108 + -337 + -503    −977

## Integers

**...More Adding Integers with Like Signs**

1. 16 + 26    42
2. -8 + -36    −44
3. 28 + 31    59
4. -121 + -93    −214
5. -622 + -881    −1,503
6. 282 + 83    365
7. -537 + -691    −1,228
8. -96 + -36    −132
9. 6,811 + 833    7,644
10. 1,832 + 16,631    18,463
11. -8,693 + -11,192    −19,885
12. 15,931 + 4,489    20,420

13. -11,121 + -16,899    −28,020
14. 37,454 + 88,697    126,151
15. -101,997 + -45,532    −147,529
16. -677,762 + -89,999    −767,761
17. 525 + 63 + 8,121    8,709
18. -18,619 + -45,697 + -21,112    −85,428
19. -18,161 + -11,132 + -6,866    −36,159
20. 682,914 + 683,319 + 51,132    1,417,365
21. 22,633 + 984,116 + 55,256    1,062,005
22. -119,194 + -83,677 + -43,288    −246,159
23. -212,201 + -48,809 + -56,009    −317,019
24. 66,683 + 102,259 + 83,387    252,329

# Answer Key

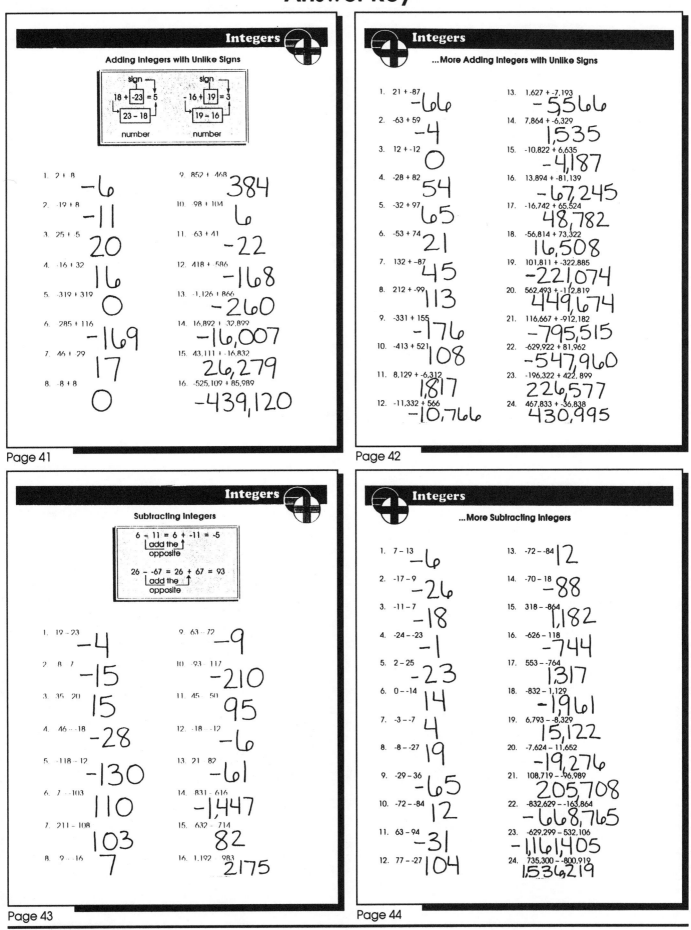

## Integers
### Adding Integers with Unlike Signs

1. 2 + 8  →  -6
2. -19 + 8  →  -11
3. 25 + 5  →  20
4. -16 + 32  →  16
5. -319 + 319  →  0
6. 285 + 116  →  -169
7. 46 + 29  →  17
8. -8 + 8  →  0
9. 852 + 468  →  384
10. -98 + 104  →  6
11. 63 + 41  →  -22
12. 418 + 586  →  -168
13. -1,126 + 866  →  -260
14. 16,892 + 32,899  →  -16,007
15. 43,111 + -16,832  →  26,279
16. -525,109 + 85,989  →  -439,120

Page 41

## Integers
### ...More Adding Integers with Unlike Signs

1. 21 + -87  →  -66
2. -63 + 59  →  -4
3. 12 + -12  →  0
4. -28 + 82  →  54
5. -32 + 97  →  65
6. -53 + 74  →  21
7. 132 + -87  →  45
8. 212 + -99  →  113
9. -331 + 155  →  -176
10. -413 + 521  →  108
11. 8,129 + -6,312  →  1,817
12. -11,332 + 566  →  -10,766
13. 1,627 + -7,193  →  -5,566
14. 7,864 + -6,329  →  1,535
15. -10,822 + 6,635  →  -4,187
16. 13,894 + -81,139  →  -67,245
17. -16,742 + 65,524  →  48,782
18. -56,814 + 73,322  →  16,508
19. 101,811 + -322,885  →  -221,074
20. 562,493 + -112,819  →  449,674
21. 116,667 + -912,182  →  -795,515
22. -629,922 + 81,962  →  -547,960
23. -196,322 + 422,899  →  226,577
24. 467,833 + -36,838  →  430,995

Page 42

## Integers
### Subtracting Integers

1. 19 - 23  →  -4
2. 8 - 7  →  -15
3. 35 - 20  →  15
4. 46 - -18  →  -28
5. -118 - 12  →  -130
6. 7 - -103  →  110
7. 211 - 108  →  103
8. 9 - -16  →  7
9. 63 - 72  →  -9
10. -93 - 117  →  -210
11. 45 - -50  →  95
12. -18 - -12  →  -6
13. 21 - 82  →  -61
14. 831 - 616  →  -1,447
15. 632 - 714  →  82
16. 1,192 - 983  →  2175

Page 43

## Integers
### ...More Subtracting Integers

1. 7 - 13  →  -6
2. -17 - 9  →  -26
3. -11 - 7  →  -18
4. -24 - -23  →  -1
5. 2 - 25  →  -23
6. 0 - -14  →  14
7. -3 - -7  →  4
8. -8 - -27  →  19
9. -29 - 36  →  -65
10. -72 - -84  →  12
11. 63 - 94  →  -31
12. 77 - -27  →  104
13. -72 - -84  →  12
14. -70 - 18  →  -88
15. 318 - -864  →  1,182
16. -626 - 118  →  -744
17. 553 - -764  →  1,317
18. -832 - 1,129  →  -1,961
19. 6,793 - -8,329  →  15,122
20. -7,624 - 11,652  →  -19,276
21. 108,719 - -96,989  →  205,708
22. -832,629 - -163,864  →  -668,765
23. -629,299 - 532,106  →  -1,161,405
24. 735,300 - 800,919  →  1,536,219

Page 44

# Answer Key

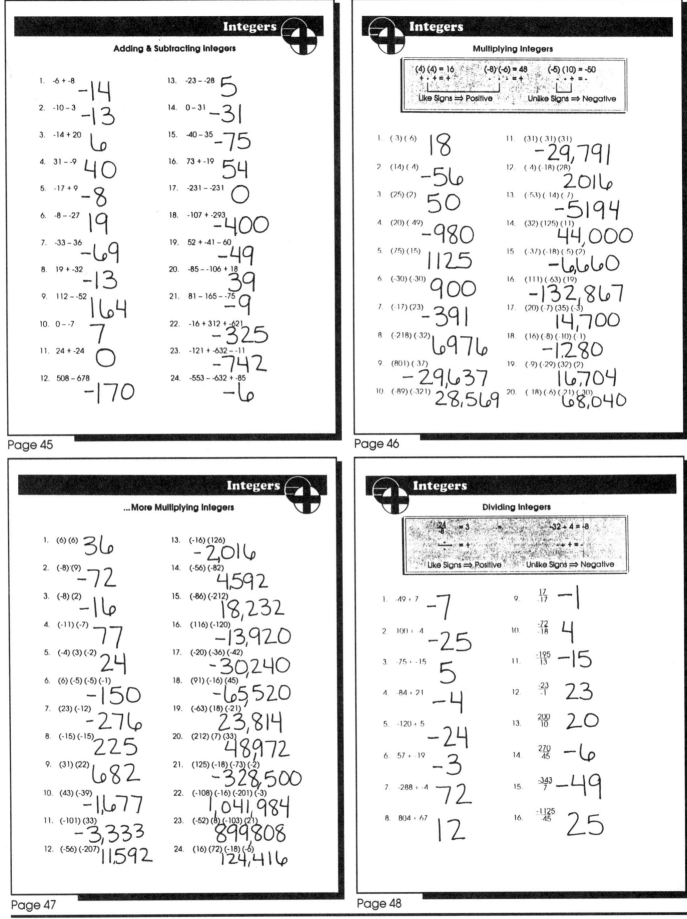

## Integers ⊕

### Adding & Subtracting Integers

1. -6 + -8  **-14**
2. -10 - 3  **-13**
3. -14 + 20  **6**
4. 31 - -9  **40**
5. -17 + 9  **-8**
6. -8 - -27  **19**
7. -33 - 36  **-69**
8. 19 + -32  **-13**
9. 112 - -52  **164**
10. 0 - -7  **7**
11. 24 + -24  **0**
12. 508 - 678  **-170**
13. -23 - -28  **5**
14. 0 - 31  **-31**
15. -40 - 35  **-75**
16. 73 + -19  **54**
17. -231 - -231  **0**
18. -107 + -293  **-400**
19. 52 + -41 - 60  **-49**
20. -85 - -106 + 18  **39**
21. 81 - 165 - -75  **-9**
22. -16 + 312 + -621  **-325**
23. -121 + -632 - -11  **-742**
24. -553 - -632 + -85  **-6**

Page 45

## ⊕ Integers

### Multiplying Integers

(4) (4) = 16   (-8) (-6) = 48   (-5) (10) = -50
**Like Signs ⟹ Positive**    **Unlike Signs ⟹ Negative**

1. (-3) ( 6)  **18**
2. (14) ( 4)  **-56**
3. (25) (2)  **50**
4. (20) ( 49)  **-980**
5. (75) (15)  **1125**
6. (-30) (-30)  **900**
7. (-17) (23)  **-391**
8. (-218) (-32)  **6976**
9. (801) ( 37)  **-29,637**
10. (-89) (-321)  **28,569**
11. (31) ( 31) (31)  **-29,791**
12. ( 4) (-18) (28)  **2016**
13. (-53) (-14) ( 7)  **-5194**
14. (32) (125) (11)  **44,000**
15. (-37) (-18) (-5) (2)  **-6,660**
16. (111) (-63) (19)  **-132,867**
17. (20) (-7) (35) (-3)  **14,700**
18. (16) (-8) (-10) (-1)  **-1,280**
19. (-9) (-29) (32) (2)  **16,704**
20. ( 18) (-6) (-21) (30)  **68,040**

Page 46

## Integers ⊕

### ...More Multiplying Integers

1. (6) (6)  **36**
2. (-8) (9)  **-72**
3. (-8) (2)  **-16**
4. (-11) (-7)  **77**
5. (-4) (3) (-2)  **24**
6. (6) (-5) (-5) (-1)  **-150**
7. (23) (-12)  **-276**
8. (-15) (-15)  **225**
9. (31) (22)  **682**
10. (43) (-39)  **-1,677**
11. (-101) (33)  **-3,333**
12. (-56) (-207)  **11,592**
13. (-16) (126)  **-2,016**
14. (-56) (-82)  **4,592**
15. (-86) (-212)  **18,232**
16. (116) (-120)  **-13,920**
17. (-20) (-36) (-42)  **-30,240**
18. (91) (-16) (45)  **-65,520**
19. (-63) (18) (-21)  **23,814**
20. (212) (7) (33)  **48,972**
21. (125) (-18) (-73) (-2)  **-328,500**
22. (-108) (-16) (-201) (-3)  **1,041,984**
23. (-52) (8) (-103) (21)  **899,808**
24. (16) (72) (-18) (-6)  **124,416**

Page 47

## ⊕ Integers

### Dividing Integers

$\frac{-24}{8}$ = -3      -32 ÷ 4 = -8
**Like Signs ⟹ Positive**    **Unlike Signs ⟹ Negative**

1. -49 ÷ 7  **-7**
2. 100 ÷ 4  **-25**
3. -75 ÷ -15  **5**
4. -84 ÷ 21  **-4**
5. -120 ÷ 5  **-24**
6. 57 ÷ -19  **-3**
7. -288 ÷ -4  **72**
8. 804 ÷ 67  **12**
9. $\frac{17}{-17}$  **-1**
10. $\frac{-72}{-18}$  **4**
11. $\frac{-195}{13}$  **-15**
12. $\frac{-23}{-1}$  **23**
13. $\frac{200}{10}$  **20**
14. $\frac{270}{-45}$  **-6**
15. $\frac{-343}{7}$  **-49**
16. $\frac{-1125}{-45}$  **25**

Page 48

# Answer Key

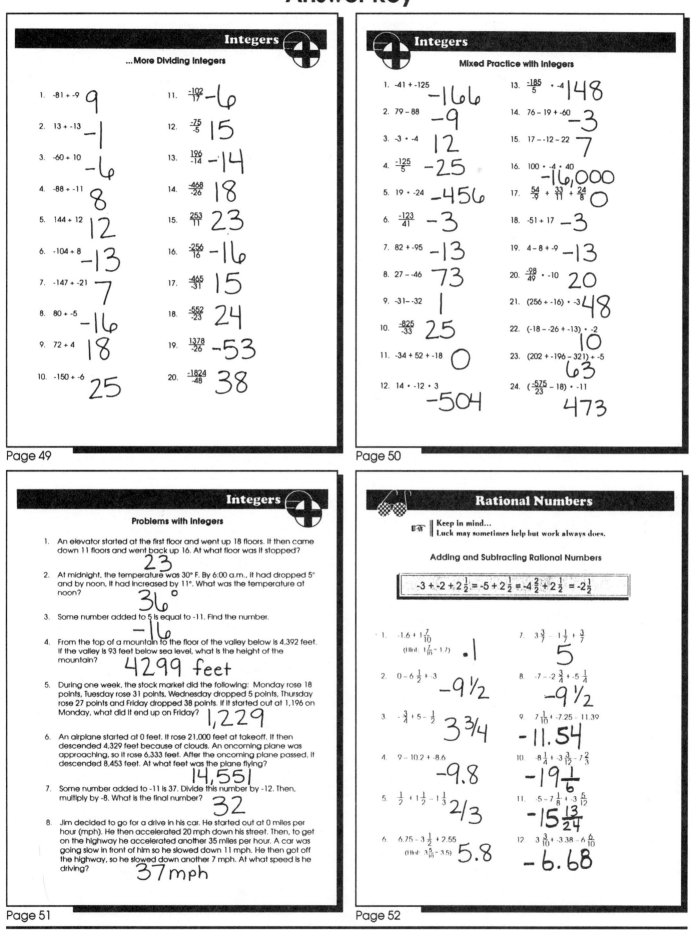

## Integers
### ...More Dividing Integers

1. -81 ÷ -9   9
2. 13 ÷ -13   -1
3. -60 ÷ 10   -6
4. -88 ÷ -11   8
5. 144 ÷ 12   12
6. -104 ÷ 8   -13
7. -147 ÷ -21   7
8. 80 ÷ -5   -16
9. 72 ÷ 4   18
10. -150 ÷ -6   25

11. $\frac{-102}{17}$   -6
12. $\frac{-75}{-5}$   15
13. $\frac{196}{-14}$   -14
14. $\frac{-468}{-26}$   18
15. $\frac{253}{11}$   23
16. $\frac{-256}{16}$   -16
17. $\frac{-465}{-31}$   15
18. $\frac{-552}{-23}$   24
19. $\frac{1378}{-26}$   -53
20. $\frac{-1824}{-48}$   38

Page 49

## Integers
### Mixed Practice with Integers

1. -41 + -125   -166
2. 79 - 88   -9
3. -3 · -4   12
4. $\frac{-125}{5}$   -25
5. 19 · -24   -456
6. $\frac{-123}{41}$   -3
7. 82 ÷ -95   -13
8. 27 - -46   73
9. -31 - -32   1
10. $\frac{-825}{-33}$   25
11. -34 + 52 + -18   0
12. 14 · -12 · 3   -504

13. $\frac{-185}{5}$ · -4   148
14. 76 - 19 + -60   -3
15. 17 - -12 - 22   7
16. 100 · -4 · 40   -16,000
17. $\frac{54}{-9} + \frac{33}{11} + \frac{24}{8}$   0
18. -51 + 17   -3
19. 4 - 8 + -9   -13
20. $\frac{-98}{49}$ · -10   20
21. (256 ÷ -16) · -3   48
22. (-18 - -26 + -13) · -2   10
23. (202 + -196 - 321) ÷ -5   63
24. ($\frac{-575}{23}$ - 18) · -11   473

Page 50

## Integers
### Problems with Integers

1. An elevator started at the first floor and went up 18 floors. It then came down 11 floors and went back up 16. At what floor was it stopped?   23

2. At midnight, the temperature was 30° F. By 6:00 a.m., it had dropped 5° and by noon, it had increased by 11°. What was the temperature at noon?   36°

3. Some number added to 5 is equal to -11. Find the number.   -16

4. From the top of a mountain to the floor of the valley below is 4,392 feet. If the valley is 93 feet below sea level, what is the height of the mountain?   4299 feet

5. During one week, the stock market did the following: Monday rose 18 points, Tuesday rose 31 points, Wednesday dropped 5 points, Thursday rose 27 points and Friday dropped 38 points. If it started out at 1,196 on Monday, what did it end up on Friday?   1,229

6. An airplane started at 0 feet. It rose 21,000 feet at takeoff. It then descended 4,329 feet because of clouds. An oncoming plane was approaching, so it rose 6,333 feet. After the oncoming plane passed, it descended 8,453 feet. At what feet was the plane flying?   14,551

7. Some number added to -11 is 37. Divide this number by -12. Then, multiply by -8. What is the final number?   32

8. Jim decided to go for a drive in his car. He started out at 0 miles per hour (mph). He then accelerated 20 mph down his street. Then, to get on the highway he accelerated another 35 miles per hour. A car was going slow in front of him so he slowed down 11 mph. He then got off the highway, so he slowed down another 7 mph. At what speed is he driving?   37mph

Page 51

## Rational Numbers

🖘 **Keep in mind...**
Luck may sometimes help but work always does.

### Adding and Subtracting Rational Numbers

$$-3 + -2 + 2\frac{1}{2} = -5 + 2\frac{1}{2} = -4\frac{2}{2} + 2\frac{1}{2} = -2\frac{1}{2}$$

1. -1.6 + 1$\frac{7}{10}$
   (Hint: 1$\frac{7}{10}$ = 1.7)   .1

2. 0 - 6$\frac{1}{2}$ + -3   -9½

3. -$\frac{3}{4}$ + 5 - $\frac{1}{2}$   3¾

4. 9 - 10.2 + -8.6   -9.8

5. $\frac{1}{2}$ + 1$\frac{1}{2}$ - 1$\frac{1}{3}$   2/3

6. 6.75 - 3$\frac{1}{2}$ + 2.55
   (Hint: 3$\frac{5}{10}$ = 3.5)   5.8

7. 3$\frac{3}{7}$ - 1$\frac{1}{7}$ + $\frac{3}{7}$   5

8. -7 - 2$\frac{3}{4}$ + -5$\frac{1}{4}$   -9½

9. 7$\frac{1}{10}$ + -7.25 - 11.39   -11.54

10. -8$\frac{1}{4}$ + -3$\frac{3}{12}$ - 7$\frac{2}{3}$   -19$\frac{1}{6}$

11. -5 - 7$\frac{1}{8}$ + -3$\frac{5}{12}$   -15$\frac{13}{24}$

12. 3$\frac{3}{10}$ + -3.38 - 6$\frac{6}{10}$   -6.68

Page 52

# Answer Key

## Rational Numbers

### ...More Adding and Subtracting Rational Numbers

1. $-3\frac{5}{10}+8$   4.5
2. $-5\frac{3}{7}+-3\frac{3}{14}$   $-8\frac{9}{14}$
3. $6\frac{1}{6}-6\frac{3}{10}$   $-\frac{2}{15}$
4. $-8+15.32$   7.32
5. $-8\frac{3}{10}--5.9$   $-2.4$
6. $13-5\frac{3}{5}$   $7\frac{2}{5}$
7. $12\frac{1}{9}+-5\frac{2}{3}$   $6\frac{4}{9}$
8. $-11.03--21.6$   10.57
9. $-7\frac{3}{10}-16.53$   $-23.83$
10. $31\frac{8}{9}+-27\frac{27}{81}$   $4\frac{5}{9}$

11. $11-18.6+-3\frac{3}{10}$   $-10.9$
12. $-5\frac{2}{10}+16.7-3\frac{1}{5}$   8.3
13. $13\frac{1}{3}+-12+-7\frac{7}{12}$   $-6\frac{1}{4}$
14. $41.32+-18.7-16.21$   6.41
15. $-18.75-5\frac{3}{4}-7\frac{5}{12}$   $-31\frac{11}{12}$
16. $-15-21\frac{1}{7}+18\frac{2}{49}$   $-18\frac{5}{49}$
17. $7\frac{2}{3}+8\frac{4}{9}+-16\frac{1}{6}$   $15\frac{7}{18}$
18. $-31.5--3\frac{7}{10}+21$   $-6.8$
19. $25\frac{1}{5}-17.3+-11\frac{2}{11}$   $-3\frac{31}{110}$
20. $19.25--6\frac{3}{4}+12\frac{5}{12}$   $38\frac{5}{12}$

## Rational Numbers

### Multiplying and Dividing Rational Numbers

$-4 \cdot 5 \cdot \frac{1}{2} = -20 \cdot \frac{1}{2} = \frac{-20}{1} \cdot \frac{1}{2} = \frac{-10}{1} = -10$

$5\frac{1}{4} \cdot 1\frac{2}{7} + 1\frac{1}{2} = \frac{21}{4} \cdot \frac{9}{7} + \frac{3}{2} = \frac{9}{2}$ or $4\frac{1}{2}$

1. $-1\frac{2}{3} \cdot -3\frac{1}{5}$   $5\frac{1}{3}$
2. $4\frac{5}{9} + -\frac{10}{27}$   $-12.3$
3. $4\frac{1}{4} \cdot 3\frac{1}{5}$   $13\frac{3}{5}$
4. $-9\frac{3}{8} + -3\frac{9}{12}$   2.5
5. $-\frac{3}{8} \cdot 4 \cdot \frac{4}{9}$   $-2/3$
6. $-9\frac{3}{5} + \frac{12}{5} \cdot -4$   16

7. $-4.1 \cdot -5.2 + 4$   5.33
8. $6.2 \cdot 3 \cdot -\frac{-1}{2}$   (Hint: $\frac{1}{2} = .5$)   $-9.3$
9. $(-2\frac{1}{2})(-2\frac{1}{2}) + .5$   12.5
10. $-\frac{6}{7} \cdot -\frac{5}{12} \cdot -\frac{2}{15}$   $-1/21$
11. $5\frac{2}{3} \cdot 9.81 \cdot 0$   0
12. $12 \cdot 3\frac{1}{4} \cdot -2\frac{2}{3}$   $-104$

## Rational Numbers

### ...More Multiplying and Dividing Rational Numbers

1. $-9\frac{3}{5} \cdot \frac{5}{12}$   $-4$
2. $-\frac{16}{7} + \frac{12}{35}$   $-6\frac{2}{3}$
3. $4\frac{1}{2} \cdot -2\frac{2}{7}$   $-10\frac{2}{7}$
4. $-5\frac{5}{6} + 2\frac{1}{3}$   $-2\frac{1}{2}$
5. $-8\frac{1}{3} \cdot -2\frac{2}{5}$   20
6. $16\frac{1}{8} + 14\frac{1}{3}$   $1\frac{1}{8}$
7. $-37.6 \cdot .03$   $-1.128$
8. $-16.188 + -4.26$   3.8
9. $-1.75 \cdot -3.4$   5.95
10. $-3.45 + 1\frac{1}{2}$   $-2\frac{3}{10}$

11. $-8 + -1\frac{1}{3} \cdot -5$   $-30$
12. $4.498 + -1.73 \cdot -1.2$   3.12
13. $-\frac{5}{7} + -\frac{1}{14} \cdot -\frac{1}{2}$   5
14. $-6\frac{2}{3} \cdot 2.75 + -1\frac{2}{3}$   11
15. $-\frac{3}{8} + -3 \cdot \frac{4}{5}$   $\frac{1}{10}$
16. $12\frac{3}{8} \cdot -2\frac{2}{3} + 2.5$   $-13.2$
17. $-\frac{5}{6} \cdot 4\frac{1}{4} \cdot -\frac{3}{5}$   $2\frac{1}{8}$
18. $-3\frac{1}{5} + 4\frac{2}{5} + -1\frac{1}{7}$   $\frac{7}{11}$
19. $3\frac{3}{5} \cdot -1.46$   $-5.256$
20. $4\frac{2}{3} + -\frac{6}{7} \cdot \frac{9}{10}$   $-4.9$

## Rational Numbers

### Order of Operations with Rational Numbers

1. $-28 + 7 + 2\frac{1}{3}$   $-1\frac{2}{3}$
2. $\frac{1}{2}(-16-4)$   $-10$
3. $-9 + -3 + 4 \cdot -\frac{-1}{4} - 20 + 5$   $-2$
4. $\frac{1}{3}((-18+3) + (5+7) + -4)$   $-6$
5. $(8\frac{1}{3} + 3\frac{2}{3}) + 4 --16$   19
6. $\frac{(80 \cdot \frac{1}{2}) + 35}{-10 + 25}$   5
7. $2(-6(3-12)-17)$   74
8. $\frac{1}{4}(20 + 72 + -9)$   3
9. $3 \cdot 2(4 + (9+3))$   42
10. $50 + ((4 \cdot 5) - (36 + 2)) + -91$   $-66$

# Answer Key

## Rational Numbers

### ...More Order of Operations with Rational Numbers

1. $2 + (48 \div (12 + 4)) - 16$ **−11**
2. $72 \div (\frac{29 + 7}{4 \cdot 3}) - (-26 + 92)$ **−42**
3. $(\frac{3(12 - 7)}{2 + 3}) \cdot 6 + 11$ **29**
4. $\frac{2((7 \cdot 3) + 6)}{26 + 13} - 8$ **19**
5. $\frac{5 + (4 \cdot 3(2 + 1)) + 4}{19 + -10}$ **5**
6. $\frac{((48 + 2)2) + 5}{2} + 16$ **26**
7. $-16 + (20 \cdot 6) \div (6 + 2) + 31$ **30**
8. $\frac{7(8 - 1) + (42 + 3)}{(10 - 7)3} + 7$ **14**
9. $35 + \frac{50 + 25}{5 \cdot 5} - (8 + 11)$ **19**
10. $(5(20 - 2)) \div \frac{30}{2} + 6 - 3$ **9**
11. $\frac{3(4(9 - 2))}{12} + (16 \cdot 3)$ **55**
12. $(\frac{(8 + 3) \cdot (16 - 7)}{3} + 11) \div 4 + 8$ **19**

Page 57

## Rational Numbers

### Comparing Rational Numbers

Use <, > or = to make a true sentence.

| | |
|---|---|
| 5.68 ____ 5.7 | $-7\frac{3}{10}$ ____ -7.29 |
| 5.68 < 5.70 | -7.30 < -7.29 |

1. 2.5 **=** $2\frac{17}{34}$
2. 1.049 **<** 1.49
3. $.\bar{3}$ **<** .3
4. 15.62 **>** 1.562
5. 8156.6 **<** 8166.6
6. $-7\frac{4}{5}$ **=** $-7\frac{24}{30}$
7. $-8\frac{7}{8}$ **<** -8.857
8. 329.93 **>** 32.993
9. 982.61 **<** 7662.8
10. $13\frac{5}{8}$ **>** 13.6

Write in descending order.

$5\frac{1}{2}, 5\frac{3}{5}, 5.4$ → Rewrite → 5.5, 5.6, 5.4 → $5\frac{3}{5}, 5\frac{1}{2}, 5.4$ Descending Order

1. 6.41, 6.411, 6.4111 — **3, 2, 1**
2. $-2\frac{9}{14}, -2\frac{5}{8}, -2\frac{4}{7}$ — **3, 2, 1**
3. $11.6, 11\frac{2}{3}, 11\frac{14}{25}$ — **2, 1, 3**
4. $-.030, -\frac{33}{100}, -.003$ — **2, 3, 1**
5. $7\frac{5}{8}, 7\frac{3}{4}, 7.775$ — **3, 2, 1**
6. $-10\frac{3}{4}, -10.82, -10\frac{2}{3}$ — **2, 3, 1**
7. $3.08, 3\frac{4}{5}, 3\frac{3}{5}$ — **3, 1, 2**
8. $-1.35, -1\frac{1}{8}, -1\frac{1}{4}$ — **3, 1, 2**

Page 58

## Rational Numbers

### The Flip dıꟽ

Perform each of the following operations on your calculator. Then flip your calculator and find the "word answer" to the questions.

1. What did Amelia Earhart's father say the first time he saw her fly an airplane?
   .115 x 3 + 10141 x 5 = **50705.345**
   Flip dıꟽ **She solos**

2. What did Farmer MacGregor throw at Peter Rabbit to chase him out of the garden?
   (27 x 109 + 4 - .027) 2 x 9 = **53045.514**
   Flip dıꟽ **his shoes**

3. What did Snoopy add to his doghouse as a result of his dogfights with the Red Baron?
   7 (3 x 303 + 50) x 8 = **53704**
   Flip dıꟽ **holes**

4. What kind of double does a golfer want to avoid at the end of a round of golf?
   4 (1956 x 4 + 153) = **31908**
   Flip dıꟽ **BOGIE**

5. What did the little girl say when she was frightened by the ghost?
   .07 x .111 x 5 + .00123 = **0.04008**
   Flip dıꟽ **BOO HOO**

Page 59

## Equations

Keep in mind...
Friends x Laughter = Lots of Joy

### Open Sentences

State the solution for each sentence.

| | |
|---|---|
| $\frac{1}{2} \cdot -10 = x$ | $\frac{-56}{-7} - 4 = z$ |
| $\frac{1}{2} \cdot \frac{-10}{1} = x$ (cancelled to $\frac{1}{1} \cdot \frac{-5}{1}$) | $8 - 4 = z$ |
| $-5 = x$ | $4 = z$ |

1. $\frac{18 + -6}{2} = a$ **6**
2. $-3 \cdot 4 - 6 = c$ **−18**
3. $4.5 - 6.2 = p$ **−1.7**
4. $\frac{-3}{8} \cdot -4 - 1 = q$ **1/2**
5. $\frac{-15 + -27}{3} = x$ **−14**
6. $-8.1 \cdot 4.2 + 16 = g$ **−18.02**
7. $\frac{1}{3} \cdot -15 + -10 = r$ **−15**
8. $1\frac{3}{5} \div \frac{16}{45} = d$ **4.5**
9. $5 \cdot 7.32 - 18.19 = n$ **18.41**
10. $\frac{3}{4} \cdot -16 + 8.12 = z$ **−3.88**
11. $\frac{-40 + 15}{5} + 6 = b$ **1**
12. $-\frac{2}{5} + \frac{4}{15} + -2\frac{1}{2} = t$ **−4**

Page 60

# Answer Key

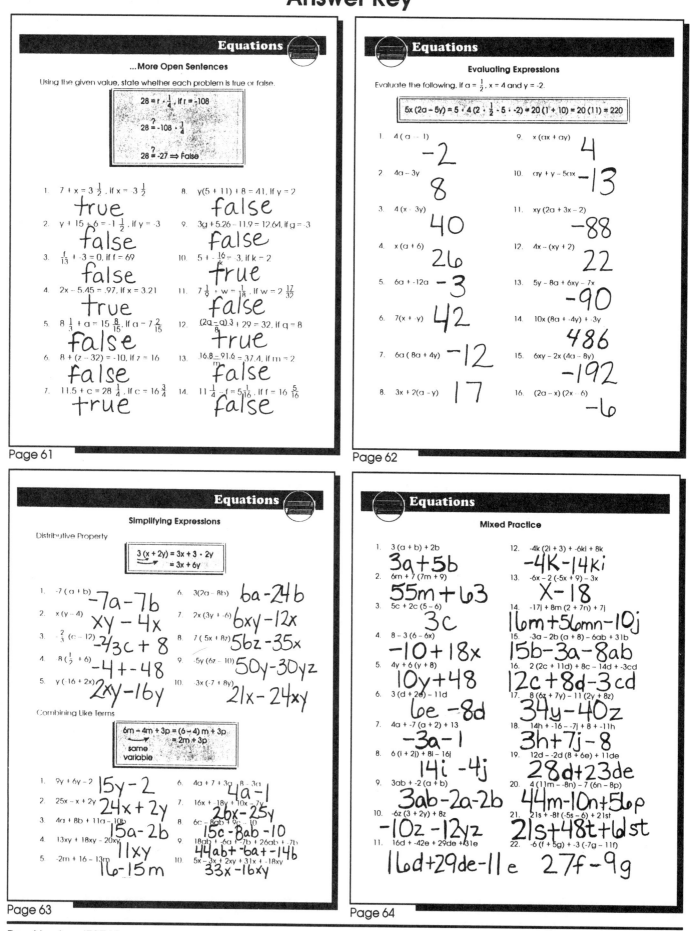

## Equations

### ...More Open Sentences

Using the given value, state whether each problem is true or false.

$$28 = r \cdot \frac{1}{4}, \text{ if } r = -108$$
$$28 \stackrel{?}{=} -108 \cdot \frac{1}{4}$$
$$28 \stackrel{?}{=} -27 \Rightarrow \text{False}$$

1. $7 + x = 3\frac{1}{2}$, if $x = -3\frac{1}{2}$ — **true**
2. $y + 15 \div 6 = -1\frac{1}{2}$, if $y = -3$ — **false**
3. $\frac{f}{13} + -3 = 0$, if $f = 69$ — **false**
4. $2x - 5.45 = .97$, if $x = 3.21$ — **true**
5. $8\frac{1}{3} + a = 15\frac{8}{15}$, if $a = 7\frac{2}{15}$ — **false**
6. $8 + (z - 32) = -10$, if $z = 16$ — **false**
7. $11.5 + c = 28\frac{1}{4}$, if $c = 16\frac{3}{4}$ — **true**

8. $y(5 + 11) + 8 = 41$, if $y = 2$ — **false**
9. $3g + 5.26 - 11.9 = 12.64$, if $g = -3$ — **false**
10. $5 + \frac{16}{k} = 3$, if $k = 2$ — **true**
11. $7\frac{1}{9} + w = \frac{1}{18}$, if $w = 2\frac{17}{32}$ — **false**
12. $(2a - q)3 + 29 = 32$, if $q = 8$ — **true**
13. $\frac{16.8 - 91.6}{m} = 37.4$, if $m = 2$ — **false**
14. $11\frac{1}{4} + -f = 5\frac{1}{16}$, if $f = 16\frac{5}{16}$ — **false**

Page 61

## Equations

### Evaluating Expressions

Evaluate the following. If $a = \frac{1}{2}$, $x = 4$ and $y = -2$.

$$5x(2a - 5y) = 5 \cdot 4(2 \cdot \frac{1}{2} - 5 \cdot -2) = 20(1 + 10) = 20(11) = 220$$

1. $4(a - 1)$ — $-2$
2. $4a - 3y$ — $8$
3. $4(x - 3y)$ — $40$
4. $x(a + 6)$ — $26$
5. $6a + -12a$ — $-3$
6. $7(x + y)$ — $42$
7. $6a(8a + 4y)$ — $-12$
8. $3x + 2(a - y)$ — $17$

9. $x(ax + ay)$ — $4$
10. $ay + y - 5ax$ — $-13$
11. $xy(2a + 3x - 2)$ — $-88$
12. $4x - (xy + 2)$ — $22$
13. $5y - 8a + 6xy - 7x$ — $-90$
14. $10x(8a + -4y) + -3y$ — $486$
15. $6xy - 2x(4a - 8y)$ — $-192$
16. $(2a - x)(2x - 6)$ — $-6$

Page 62

## Equations

### Simplifying Expressions

Distributive Property

$$3(x + 2y) = 3x + 3 \cdot 2y = 3x + 6y$$

1. $-7(a + b)$ — $-7a - 7b$
2. $x(y - 4)$ — $xy - 4x$
3. $-\frac{2}{3}(c - 12)$ — $-\frac{2}{3}c + 8$
4. $8(\frac{1}{2} + 6)$ — $-4 + -48$
5. $y(-16 + 2x)$ — $2xy - 16y$

6. $3(2a - 8b)$ — $6a - 24b$
7. $2x(3y - 6)$ — $6xy - 12x$
8. $7(5x + 8z)$ — $56z - 35x$
9. $-5y(6z - 10)$ — $50y - 30yz$
10. $-3x(-7 + 8y)$ — $21x - 24xy$

Combining Like Terms

$$6m - 4m + 3p = (6 - 4)m + 3p = 2m + 3p$$

same variable

1. $9y + 6y - 2$ — $15y - 2$
2. $25x - x + 2y$ — $24x + 2y$
3. $4a + 8b + 11a - 10b$ — $15a - 2b$
4. $13xy + 18xy - 20xy$ — $11xy$
5. $-2m + 16 - 13m$ — $16 - 15m$

6. $4a + 7 + 3a - 8 - 3a$ — $4a - 1$
7. $16x - 18y + 10x - 7y$ — $26x - 25y$
8. $6c - 8ab + 9c - 3c - 10$ — $15c - 8ab - 10$
9. $18ab + -6a - 7b + 26ab + -7b$ — $44ab + -6a + -14b$
10. $5x - 3x + 2xy + 31x + -18xy$ — $33x - 16xy$

Page 63

## Equations

### Mixed Practice

1. $3(a + b) + 2b$ — $3a + 5b$
2. $6m + 7(7m + 9)$ — $55m + 63$
3. $5c + 2c(5 - 6)$ — $3c$
4. $8 - 3(6 - 6x)$ — $-10 + 18x$
5. $4y + 6(y + 8)$ — $10y + 48$
6. $3(d + 2e) - 11d$ — $6e - 8d$
7. $4a + -7(a + 2) + 13$ — $-3a - 1$
8. $6(i + 2j) + 8i - 10j$ — $14i - 4j$
9. $3ab + -2(a + b)$ — $3ab - 2a - 2b$
10. $-6z(3 + 2y) + 8z$ — $-10z - 12yz$
11. $16d + -42e + 29de + 31e$ — $16d + 29de - 11e$

12. $-4k(2i + 3) + -6ki + 8k$ — $-4k - 14ki$
13. $-6x - 2(-5x + 9) - 3x$ — $x - 18$
14. $-17j + 8m(2 + 7n) + 7j$ — $16m + 56mn - 10j$
15. $-3a - 2b(a + 8) - 6ab + 31b$ — $15b - 3a - 8ab$
16. $2(2c + 11d) + 8c - 14d + -3cd$ — $12c + 8d - 3cd$
17. $8(6z + 7y) - 11(2y + 8z)$ — $34y - 40z$
18. $14h + -16 - 7j + 8 + -11h$ — $3h + 7j - 8$
19. $12d - 2d(8 + 6e) + 11de$ — $28d + 23de$
20. $4(11m - 8n) - 7(6n - 8p)$ — $44m - 10n + 56p$
21. $21s - 8t(-5s - 6) + 21st$ — $21s + 48t + 61st$
22. $-6(f + 5g) + -3(-7g - 11f)$ — $27f - 9g$

Page 64

# Answer Key

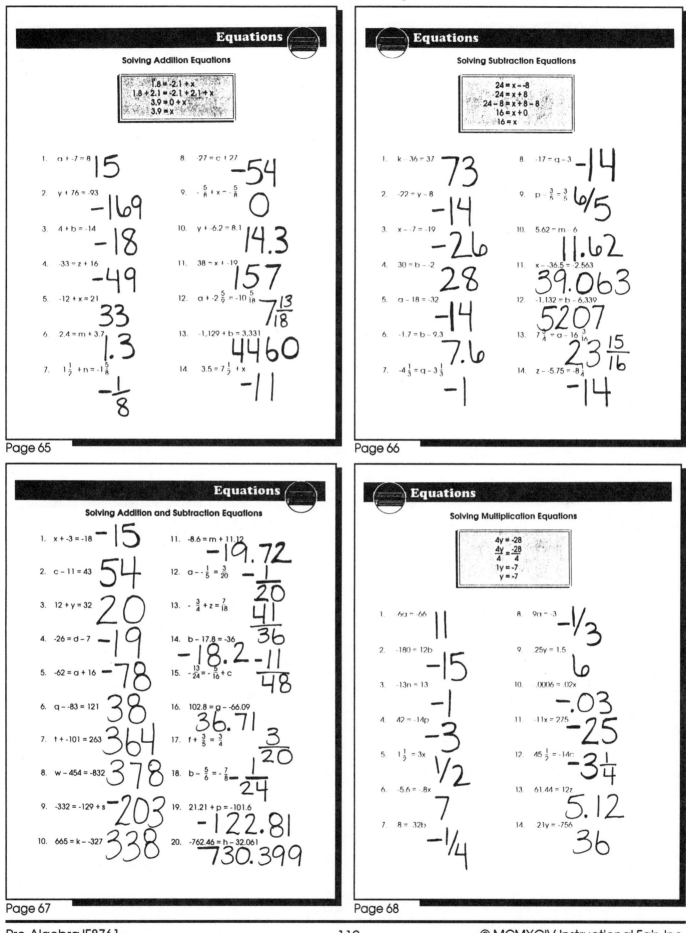

## Equations

### Solving Addition Equations

$$1.8 = -2.1 + x$$
$$1.8 + 2.1 = -2.1 + 2.1 + x$$
$$3.9 = 0 + x$$
$$3.9 = x$$

1. $a + -7 = 8$   **15**
2. $y + 76 = -93$   **-169**
3. $4 + b = -14$   **-18**
4. $-33 = z + 16$   **-49**
5. $-12 + x = 21$   **33**
6. $2.4 = m + 3.7$   **1.3**
7. $1\frac{1}{2} + n = -1\frac{5}{8}$   **$-\frac{1}{8}$**

8. $-27 = c + 27$   **-54**
9. $-\frac{5}{8} + x = -\frac{5}{8}$   **0**
10. $y + -6.2 = 8.1$   **14.3**
11. $38 = x + -19$   **157**
12. $a + -2\frac{5}{9} = -10\frac{5}{18}$   **$7\frac{13}{18}$**
13. $-1,129 + b = 3,331$   **4460**
14. $3.5 = 7\frac{1}{2} + x$   **-11**

Page 65

### Solving Subtraction Equations

$$24 = x - -8$$
$$24 = x + 8$$
$$24 - 8 = x + 8 - 8$$
$$16 = x + 0$$
$$16 = x$$

1. $k - 36 = 37$   **73**
2. $-22 = y - 8$   **-14**
3. $x - -7 = -19$   **-26**
4. $30 = b - -2$   **28**
5. $a - 18 = -32$   **-14**
6. $-1.7 = b - 9.3$   **7.6**
7. $-4\frac{1}{3} = q - 3\frac{1}{3}$   **-1**

8. $-17 = q - 3$   **-14**
9. $p - \frac{3}{5} = \frac{3}{5}$   **6/5**
10. $5.62 = m - 6$   **11.62**
11. $x - -36.5 = -2.563$   **39.063**
12. $-1.132 = b - 6,339$   **5207**
13. $7\frac{3}{4} = a - 16\frac{3}{16}$   **$23\frac{15}{16}$**
14. $z - -5.75 = -8\frac{1}{4}$   **-14**

Page 66

### Solving Addition and Subtraction Equations

1. $x + -3 = -18$   **-15**
2. $c - 11 = 43$   **54**
3. $12 + y = 32$   **20**
4. $-26 = d - 7$   **-19**
5. $-62 = a + 16$   **-78**
6. $q - -83 = 121$   **38**
7. $t + -101 = 263$   **364**
8. $w - 454 = -832$   **378**
9. $-332 = -129 + s$   **-203**
10. $665 = k - -327$   **338**

11. $-8.6 = m + 11.12$   **-19.72**
12. $a - -\frac{1}{5} = \frac{3}{20}$   **$-\frac{1}{20}$**
13. $-\frac{3}{4} + z = \frac{7}{18}$   **$\frac{41}{36}$**
14. $b - 17.8 = -36$   **-18.2**
15. $-\frac{13}{24} = -\frac{5}{16} + c$   **$-\frac{11}{48}$**
16. $102.8 = g - -66.09$   **36.71**
17. $f + \frac{3}{5} = \frac{3}{4}$   **$\frac{3}{20}$**
18. $b - \frac{5}{6} = -\frac{7}{8}$   **$-\frac{1}{24}$**
19. $21.21 + p = -101.6$   **-122.81**
20. $-762.46 = h - 32.061$   **730.399**

Page 67

### Solving Multiplication Equations

$$4y = -28$$
$$\frac{4y}{4} = \frac{-28}{4}$$
$$1y = -7$$
$$y = -7$$

1. $-6a = -66$   **11**
2. $-180 = 12b$   **-15**
3. $-13n = 13$   **-1**
4. $42 = -14p$   **-3**
5. $1\frac{1}{2} = 3x$   **1/2**
6. $-5.6 = -.8x$   **7**
7. $8 = -32b$   **-1/4**

8. $9a = -3$   **-1/3**
9. $.25y = 1.5$   **6**
10. $.0006 = .02x$   **-.03**
11. $-11x = 275$   **-25**
12. $45\frac{1}{2} = -14c$   **$-3\frac{1}{4}$**
13. $61.44 = 12z$   **5.12**
14. $21y = -756$   **36**

Page 68

# Answer Key

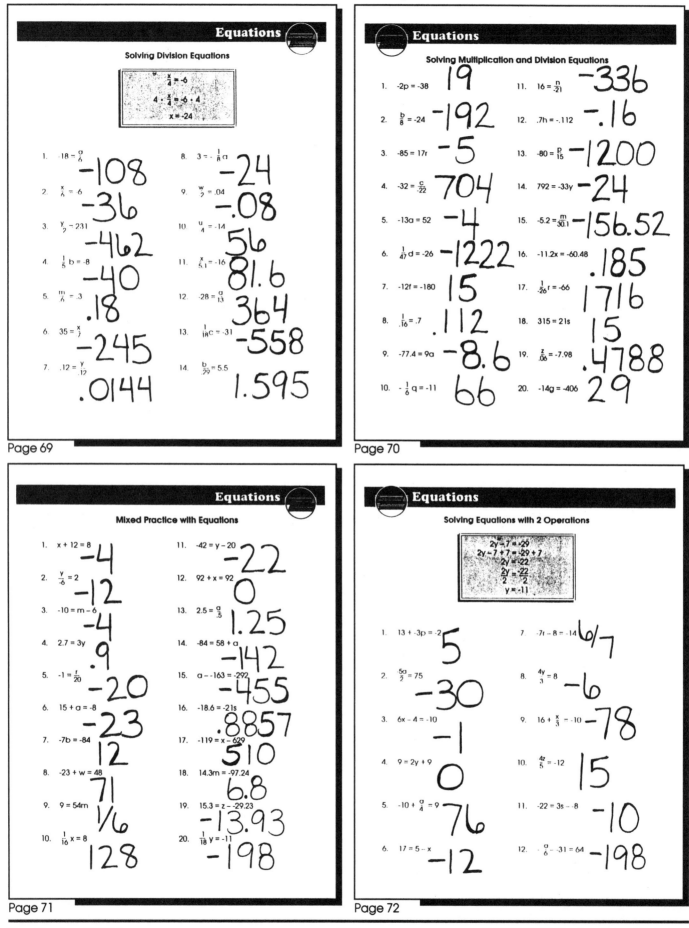

## Equations

### Solving Division Equations

1. $-18 = \frac{a}{6}$   **-108**
2. $\frac{x}{6} = 6$   **-36**
3. $\frac{y}{2} = 231$   **-462**
4. $\frac{1}{5}b = -8$   **-40**
5. $\frac{m}{6} = .3$   **.18**
6. $35 = \frac{x}{7}$   **-245**
7. $.12 = \frac{y}{.12}$   **.0144**

8. $3 = -\frac{1}{8}a$   **-24**
9. $\frac{w}{2} = .04$   **-.08**
10. $\frac{u}{4} = -14$   **56**
11. $\frac{x}{5.1} = -16$   **81.6**
12. $-28 = \frac{a}{13}$   **364**
13. $\frac{1}{18}c = -31$   **-558**
14. $\frac{b}{.29} = 5.5$   **1.595**

Page 69

## Equations

### Solving Multiplication and Division Equations

1. $-2p = -38$   **19**
2. $\frac{b}{8} = -24$   **-192**
3. $-85 = 17r$   **-5**
4. $-32 = \frac{c}{-22}$   **704**
5. $-13a = 52$   **-4**
6. $\frac{1}{47}d = -26$   **-1222**
7. $-12f = -180$   **15**
8. $\frac{1}{.16} = .7$   **.112**
9. $-77.4 = 9a$   **-8.6**
10. $-\frac{1}{6}q = -11$   **66**

11. $16 = \frac{n}{-21}$   **-336**
12. $.7h = -.112$   **-.16**
13. $-80 = \frac{p}{15}$   **-1200**
14. $792 = -33y$   **-24**
15. $-5.2 = \frac{m}{30.1}$   **-156.52**
16. $-11.2x = -60.48$   **.185**
17. $\frac{1}{-26}r = -66$   **1716**
18. $315 = 21s$   **15**
19. $\frac{z}{.06} = -7.98$   **.4788**
20. $-14g = -406$   **29**

Page 70

## Equations

### Mixed Practice with Equations

1. $x + 12 = 8$   **-4**
2. $\frac{y}{-6} = 2$   **-12**
3. $-10 = m - 6$   **-4**
4. $2.7 = 3y$   **.9**
5. $-1 = \frac{r}{20}$   **-20**
6. $15 + a = -8$   **-23**
7. $-7b = -84$   **12**
8. $-23 + w = 48$   **71**
9. $9 = 54m$   **1/6**
10. $\frac{1}{16}x = 8$   **128**

11. $-42 = y - 20$   **-22**
12. $92 + x = 92$   **0**
13. $2.5 = \frac{a}{.5}$   **1.25**
14. $-84 = 58 + a$   **-142**
15. $a - -163 = -292$   **-455**
16. $-18.6 = -21s$   **.8857**
17. $-119 = x - 629$   **510**
18. $14.3m = -97.24$   **6.8**
19. $15.3 = z - -29.23$   **-13.93**
20. $\frac{1}{18}y = -11$   **-198**

Page 71

## Equations

### Solving Equations with 2 Operations

1. $13 + -3p = -2$   **5**
2. $\frac{-5a}{2} = 75$   **-30**
3. $6x - 4 = -10$   **-1**
4. $9 = 2y + 9$   **0**
5. $-10 + \frac{a}{4} = 9$   **76**
6. $17 = 5 - x$   **-12**

7. $-7r - 8 = -14$   **6/7**
8. $\frac{4y}{3} = 8$   **-6**
9. $16 + \frac{x}{3} = -10$   **-78**
10. $\frac{4z}{5} = -12$   **15**
11. $-22 = 3s - -8$   **-10**
12. $\frac{a}{6} - 31 = 64$   **-198**

Page 72

# Answer Key

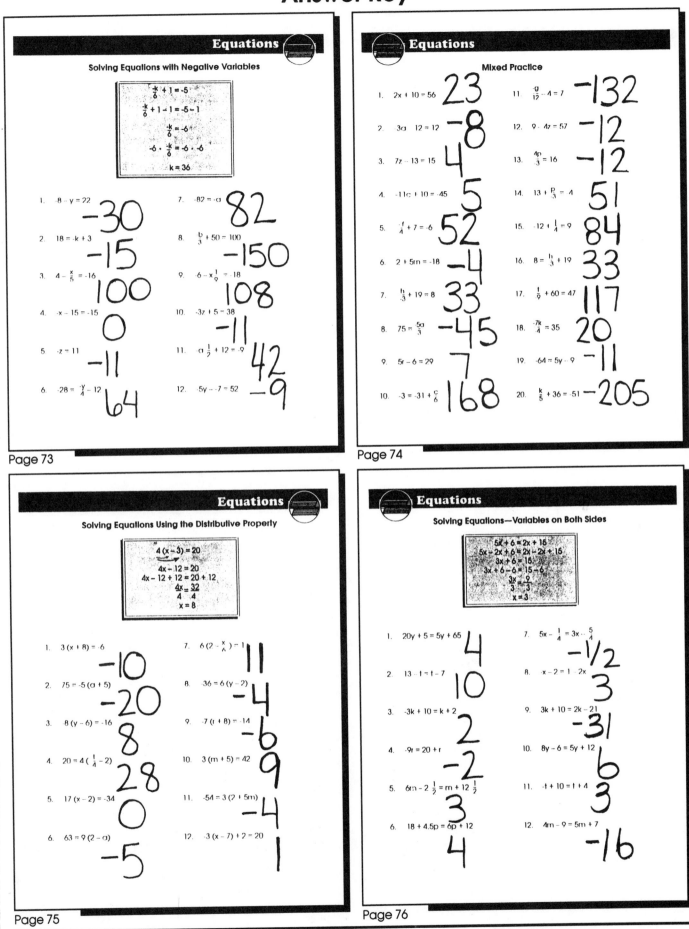

## Equations

### Solving Equations with Negative Variables

$$\frac{-k}{6} + 1 = -5$$
$$\frac{-k}{6} + 1 - 1 = -5 - 1$$
$$\frac{-k}{6} = -6$$
$$-6 \cdot \frac{-k}{6} = -6 \cdot -6$$
$$k = 36$$

1. $-8 - y = 22$ **-30**

2. $18 = -k + 3$ **-15**

3. $4 - \frac{x}{5} = -16$ **100**

4. $-x - 15 = -15$ **0**

5. $-z = 11$ **-11**

6. $-28 = \frac{y}{4} - 12$ **64**

7. $-82 = -a$ **82**

8. $\frac{b}{3} + 50 = 100$ **-150**

9. $6 - x\frac{1}{9} = 18$ **108**

10. $-3z + 5 = 38$ **-11**

11. $a\frac{1}{2} + 12 = -9$ **42**

12. $-5y - 7 = 52$ **-9**

Page 73

## Equations

### Mixed Practice

1. $2x + 10 = 56$ **23**

2. $3a - 12 = 12$ **-8**

3. $7z - 13 = 15$ **4**

4. $-11c + 10 = -45$ **5**

5. $\frac{-f}{4} + 7 = -6$ **52**

6. $2 + 5m = -18$ **-4**

7. $\frac{h}{3} + 19 = 8$ **33**

8. $75 = \frac{-5a}{3}$ **-45**

9. $5r - 6 = 29$ **7**

10. $-3 = -31 + \frac{c}{6}$ **168**

11. $\frac{-g}{12} - 4 = 7$ **-132**

12. $9 - 4z = 57$ **-12**

13. $\frac{4p}{3} = 16$ **-12**

14. $13 + \frac{p}{3} = 4$ **51**

15. $-12 + \frac{j}{4} = 9$ **84**

16. $8 = \frac{h}{3} + 19$ **33**

17. $\frac{j}{9} + 60 = 47$ **117**

18. $\frac{-7k}{4} = 35$ **20**

19. $-64 = 5y - 9$ **-11**

20. $\frac{k}{5} + 36 = -51$ **-205**

Page 74

## Equations

### Solving Equations Using the Distributive Property

$$4(x - 3) = 20$$
$$4x - 12 = 20$$
$$4x - 12 + 12 = 20 + 12$$
$$\frac{4x}{4} = \frac{32}{4}$$
$$x = 8$$

1. $3(x + 8) = -6$ **-10**

2. $75 = -5(a + 5)$ **-20**

3. $8(y - 6) = -16$ **8**

4. $20 = 4(\frac{j}{4} - 2)$ **28**

5. $17(x - 2) = -34$ **0**

6. $63 = 9(2 - a)$ **-5**

7. $6(2 - \frac{x}{4}) = 1$ **11**

8. $-36 = 6(y - 2)$ **-4**

9. $-7(t + 8) = -14$ **-6**

10. $3(m + 5) = 42$ **9**

11. $-54 = 3(2 + 5m)$ **-4**

12. $-3(x - 7) + 2 = 20$ **1**

Page 75

## Equations

### Solving Equations—Variables on Both Sides

$$5x + 6 = 2x + 15$$
$$5x - 2x + 6 = 2x - 2x + 15$$
$$3x + 6 = 15$$
$$3x + 6 - 6 = 15 - 6$$
$$\frac{3x}{3} = \frac{9}{3}$$
$$x = 3$$

1. $20y + 5 = 5y + 65$ **4**

2. $13 - t = t - 7$ **10**

3. $-3k + 10 = k + 2$ **2**

4. $-9r = 20 + r$ **-2**

5. $6m - 2\frac{1}{2} = m + 12\frac{1}{2}$ **3**

6. $18 + 4.5p = 6p + 12$ **4**

7. $5x - \frac{1}{4} = 3x - \frac{5}{4}$ **-1/2**

8. $-x - 2 = 1 - 2x$ **3**

9. $3k + 10 = 2k - 21$ **-31**

10. $8y - 6 = 5y + 12$ **6**

11. $-t + 10 = t + 4$ **3**

12. $4m - 9 = 5m + 7$ **-16**

Page 76

# Answer Key

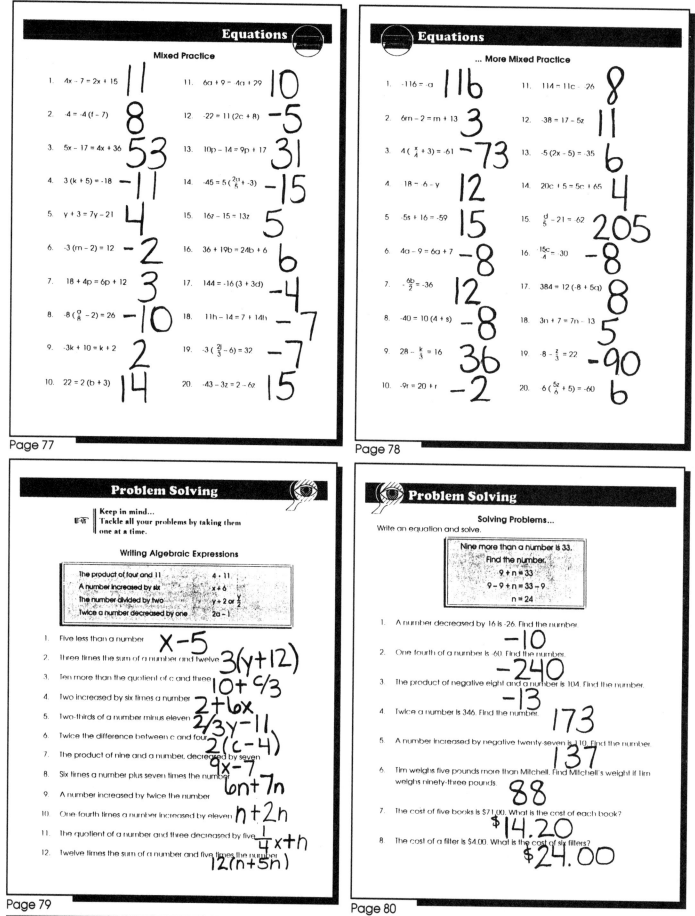

## Equations
### Mixed Practice

1. $4x - 7 = 2x + 15$ — **11**
2. $-4 = -4(f - 7)$ — **8**
3. $5x - 17 = 4x + 36$ — **53**
4. $3(k + 5) = -18$ — **-11**
5. $y + 3 = 7y - 21$ — **4**
6. $-3(m - 2) = 12$ — **-2**
7. $18 + 4p = 6p + 12$ — **3**
8. $-8(\frac{a}{8} - 2) = 26$ — **-10**
9. $-3k + 10 = k + 2$ — **2**
10. $22 = 2(b + 3)$ — **14**
11. $6a + 9 - 4a + 29$ — **10**
12. $-22 = 11(2c + 8)$ — **-5**
13. $10p - 14 = 9p + 17$ — **31**
14. $-45 = 5(\frac{2a}{5} + -3)$ — **-15**
15. $16z - 15 = 13z$ — **5**
16. $36 + 19b = 24b + 6$ — **6**
17. $144 = -16(3 + 3d)$ — **-4**
18. $11h - 14 = 7 + 14h$ — **-7**
19. $-3(\frac{2j}{3} - 6) = 32$ — **-7**
20. $-43 - 3z = 2 - 6z$ — **15**

**Page 77**

## Equations
### ... More Mixed Practice

1. $-116 = -a$ — **116**
2. $6m - 2 = m + 13$ — **3**
3. $4(\frac{x}{4} + 3) = -61$ — **-73**
4. $18 - -6 - y$ — **12**
5. $-5s + 16 = -59$ — **15**
6. $4a - 9 = 6a + 7$ — **-8**
7. $-\frac{6b}{2} = -36$ — **12**
8. $-40 = 10(4 + s)$ — **-8**
9. $28 - \frac{k}{3} = 16$ — **36**
10. $-9r = 20 + r$ — **-2**
11. $114 = 11c - -26$ — **8**
12. $-38 = 17 - 5z$ — **11**
13. $-5(2x - 5) = -35$ — **6**
14. $20c + 5 = 5c + 65$ — **4**
15. $\frac{d}{5} - 21 = -62$ — **-205**
16. $\frac{-15c}{4} = -30$ — **-8**
17. $384 = 12(-8 + 5q)$ — **8**
18. $3n + 7 = 7n - 13$ — **5**
19. $-8 - \frac{z}{3} = 22$ — **-90**
20. $6(\frac{5z}{6} + 5) = -60$ — **6**

**Page 78**

## Problem Solving

☞ **Keep in mind...**
Tackle all your problems by taking them
one at a time.

### Writing Algebraic Expressions

| | |
|---|---|
| The product of four and 11 | $4 \cdot 11$ |
| A number increased by six | $x + 6$ |
| The number divided by two | $y + 2$ or $\frac{y}{2}$ |
| Twice a number decreased by one | $2a - 1$ |

1. Five less than a number — $x - 5$
2. Three times the sum of a number and twelve — $3(y + 12)$
3. Ten more than the quotient of c and three — $10 + c/3$
4. Two increased by six times a number — $2 + 6x$
5. Two-thirds of a number minus eleven — $\frac{2}{3}y - 11$
6. Twice the difference between c and four — $2(c - 4)$
7. The product of nine and a number, decreased by seven — $9x - 7$
8. Six times a number plus seven times the number — $6n + 7n$
9. A number increased by twice the number — $n + 2n$
10. One-fourth times a number increased by eleven — 
11. The quotient of a number and three decreased by five — $\frac{1}{4}x + n$
12. Twelve times the sum of a number and five times the number — $12(n + 5n)$

**Page 79**

## Problem Solving
### Solving Problems...

Write an equation and solve.

| |
|---|
| Nine more than a number is 33. |
| Find the number. |
| $9 + n = 33$ |
| $9 - 9 + n = 33 - 9$ |
| $n = 24$ |

1. A number decreased by 16 is -26. Find the number. — **-10**
2. One fourth of a number is -60. Find the number. — **-240**
3. The product of negative eight and a number is 104. Find the number. — **-13**
4. Twice a number is 346. Find the number. — **173**
5. A number increased by negative twenty-seven is 110. Find the number. — **137**
6. Tim weighs five pounds more than Mitchell. Find Mitchell's weight if Tim weighs ninety-three pounds. — **88**
7. The cost of five books is $71.00. What is the cost of each book? — **$14.20**
8. The cost of a filter is $4.00. What is the cost of six filters? — **$24.00**

**Page 80**

# Answer Key

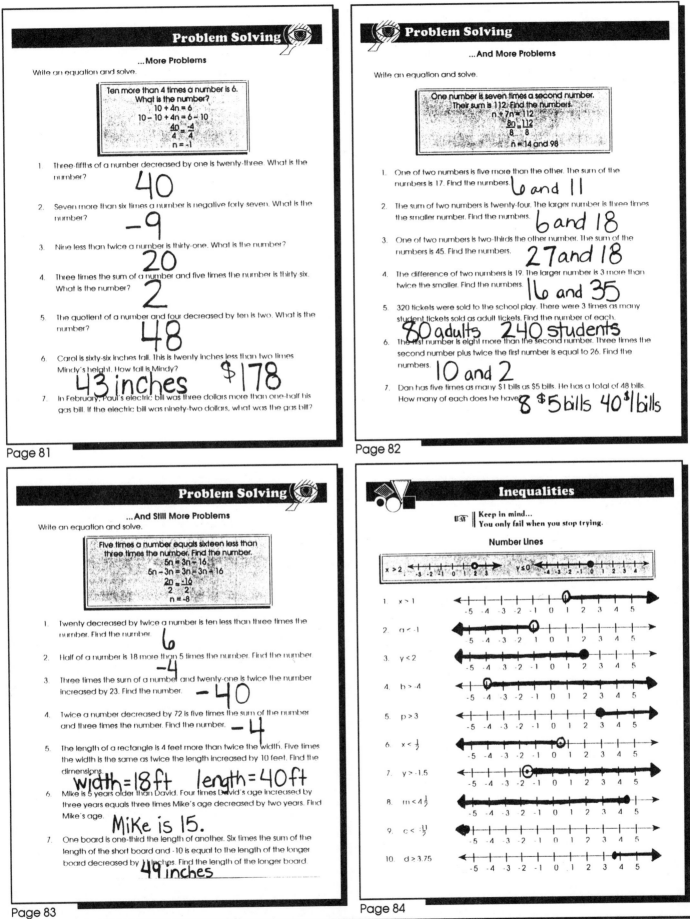

## Problem Solving
### ...More Problems

Write an equation and solve.

> Ten more than 4 times a number is 6.
> What is the number?
> $10 + 4n = 6$
> $10 - 10 + 4n = 6 - 10$
> $\frac{4n}{4} = \frac{-4}{4}$
> $n = -1$

1.  Three-fifths of a number decreased by one is twenty-three. What is the number?

    **40**

2.  Seven more than six times a number is negative forty-seven. What is the number?

    **-9**

3.  Nine less than twice a number is thirty-one. What is the number?

    **20**

4.  Three times the sum of a number and five times the number is thirty-six. What is the number?

    **2**

5.  The quotient of a number and four decreased by ten is two. What is the number?

    **48**

6.  Carol is sixty-six inches tall. This is twenty inches less than two times Mindy's height. How tall is Mindy?

    **43 inches**

7.  In February, Paul's electric bill was three dollars more than one-half his gas bill. If the electric bill was ninety-two dollars, what was the gas bill?

    **$178**

Page 81

## Problem Solving
### ...And More Problems

Write an equation and solve.

> One number is seven times a second number.
> Their sum is 112. Find the numbers.
> $n + 7n = 112$
> $\frac{8n}{8} = \frac{112}{8}$
> $n = 14$ and $98$

1.  One of two numbers is five more than the other. The sum of the numbers is 17. Find the numbers.

    **6 and 11**

2.  The sum of two numbers is twenty-four. The larger number is three times the smaller number. Find the numbers.

    **6 and 18**

3.  One of two numbers is two-thirds the other number. The sum of the numbers is 45. Find the numbers.

    **27 and 18**

4.  The difference of two numbers is 19. The larger number is 3 more than twice the smaller. Find the numbers.

    **16 and 35**

5.  320 tickets were sold to the school play. There were 3 times as many student tickets sold as adult tickets. Find the number of each.

    **80 adults    240 students**

6.  The first number is eight more than the second number. Three times the second number plus twice the first number is equal to 26. Find the numbers.

    **10 and 2**

7.  Dan has five times as many $1 bills as $5 bills. He has a total of 48 bills. How many of each does he have?

    **8 $5 bills    40 $1 bills**

Page 82

## Problem Solving
### ...And Still More Problems

Write an equation and solve.

> Five times a number equals sixteen less than three times the number. Find the number.
> $5n = 3n - 16$
> $5n - 3n = 3n - 3n - 16$
> $\frac{2n}{2} = \frac{-16}{2}$
> $n = -8$

1.  Twenty decreased by twice a number is ten less than three times the number. Find the number.

    **6**

2.  Half of a number is 18 more than 5 times the number. Find the number.

    **-4**

3.  Three times the sum of a number and twenty-one is twice the number increased by 23. Find the number.

    **-40**

4.  Twice a number decreased by 72 is five times the sum of the number and three times the number. Find the number.

    **-4**

5.  The length of a rectangle is 4 feet more than twice the width. Five times the width is the same as twice the length increased by 10 feet. Find the dimensions.

    **width = 18 ft    length = 40 ft**

6.  Mike is 5 years older than David. Four times David's age increased by three years equals three times Mike's age decreased by two years. Find Mike's age.

    **Mike is 15.**

7.  One board is one-third the length of another. Six times the sum of the length of the short board and -10 is equal to the length of the longer board decreased by 11 inches. Find the length of the longer board.

    **49 inches**

Page 83

## Inequalities

☞ Keep in mind...
You only fail when you stop trying.

### Number Lines

| $x > 2$ | $y \leq 0$ |

1. $x > 1$

2. $a < -1$

3. $y < 2$

4. $b > -4$

5. $p > 3$

6. $x < \frac{1}{2}$

7. $y > -1.5$

8. $m < 4\frac{1}{2}$

9. $c < -\frac{11}{2}$

10. $d > 3.75$

Page 84

123

# Answer Key

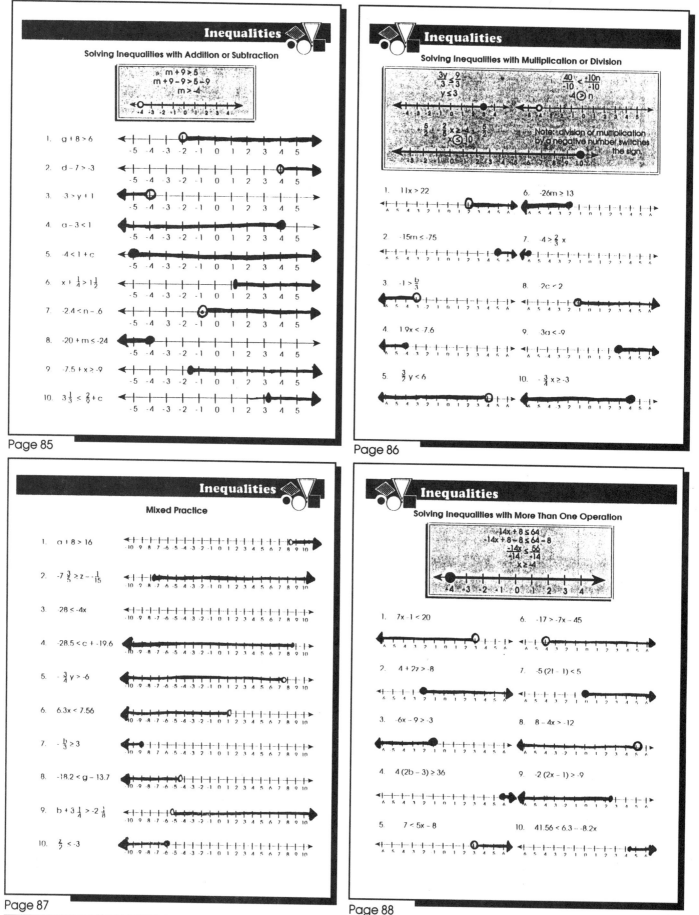

## Inequalities
### Solving Inequalities with Addition or Subtraction

$m + 9 > 5$
$m + 9 - 9 > 5 - 9$
$m > -4$

1. $g + 8 > 6$
2. $d - 7 > -3$
3. $3 > y + 1$
4. $a - 3 < 1$
5. $-4 < 1 + c$
6. $x + \frac{1}{4} > 1\frac{1}{2}$
7. $-2.4 < n - .6$
8. $-20 + m \le -24$
9. $-7.5 + x \ge -9$
10. $3\frac{1}{3} < \frac{2}{9} + c$

Page 85

## Inequalities
### Solving Inequalities with Multiplication or Division

$\frac{3y}{3} \le \frac{9}{3}$
$y \le 3$

$\frac{-40}{-10} < \frac{-10n}{-10}$
$-4 > n$

Note: division or multiplication by a negative number switches the sign.

1. $11x > 22$
2. $-15m \le -75$
3. $-1 > \frac{b}{3}$
4. $1.9x < -7.6$
5. $\frac{3}{2}y < 6$
6. $-26m \ge 13$
7. $-4 > \frac{2}{3}x$
8. $2c < 2$
9. $3a < -9$
10. $-\frac{3}{4}x \ge -3$

Page 86

## Inequalities
### Mixed Practice

1. $a + 8 > 16$
2. $-7\frac{3}{5} > z - \frac{1}{15}$
3. $-28 < -4x$
4. $-28.5 < c + -19.6$
5. $-\frac{3}{4}y > -6$
6. $6.3x < 7.56$
7. $-\frac{b}{3} \ge 3$
8. $-18.2 < g - 13.7$
9. $b + 3\frac{1}{4} > -2\frac{1}{8}$
10. $\frac{z}{2} < -3$

Page 87

## Inequalities
### Solving Inequalities with More Than One Operation

$-14x + 8 \le 64$
$-14x + 8 - 8 \le 64 - 8$
$\frac{-14x}{-14} \le \frac{56}{-14}$
$x \ge -4$

1. $7x - 1 < 20$
2. $4 + 2z > -8$
3. $-6x - 9 > -3$
4. $4(2b - 3) \ge 36$
5. $7 < 5x - 8$
6. $-17 > -7x - 45$
7. $-5(2t - 1) < 5$
8. $8 - 4x > -12$
9. $-2(2x - 1) > -9$
10. $41.56 < 6.3 - -8.2x$

Page 88

# Answer Key

## Inequalities
### Solving Inequalities with Variables on Both Sides

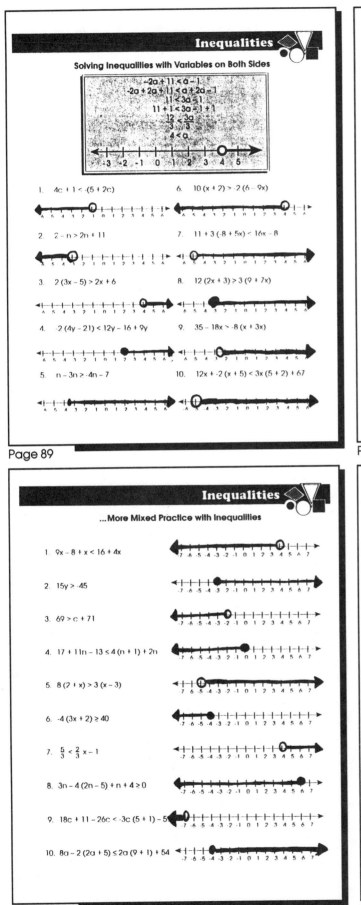

**Page 89**

## Inequalities
### Mixed Practice with Inequalities

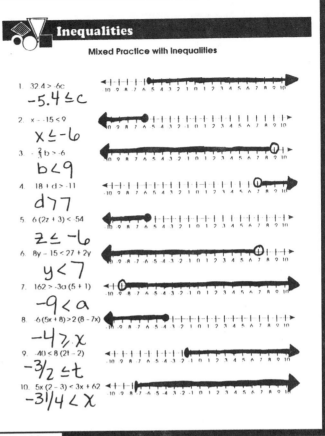

1. $32.4 > -6c$

$-5.4 \le c$

2. $x - -15 < 9$

$x \le -6$

3. $-\frac{2}{3}b > -6$

$b < 9$

4. $18 + d > -11$

$d > 7$

5. $6(2z + 3) < -54$

$z \le -6$

6. $8y - 15 < 27 + 2y$

$y < 7$

7. $162 > -3a(5 + 1)$

$-9 < a$

8. $-6(5x + 8) > 2(8 - 7x)$

$-4 \ge x$

9. $-40 < 8(2t - 2)$

$-\frac{3}{2} \le t$

10. $5x(2 - 3) > 3x + 62$

$-31/4 < x$

**Page 90**

## Inequalities
### ...More Mixed Practice with Inequalities

1. $9x - 8 + x < 16 + 4x$

2. $15y > -45$

3. $69 > c + 71$

4. $17 + 11n - 13 < 4(n + 1) + 2n$

5. $8(2 + x) > 3(x - 3)$

6. $-4(3x + 2) \ge 40$

7. $\frac{5}{3} < \frac{2}{3}x - 1$

8. $3n - 4(2n - 5) + n + 4 > 0$

9. $18c + 11 - 26c < -3c(5 + 1) - 5$

10. $8a - 2(2a + 5) \le 2a(9 + 1) + 54$

**Page 91**

## Inequalities
### A Logical Conclusion

Mike, Dale, Paul and Charlie are the athletic director, quarterback, pitcher and goalie, but not necessarily in that order. From these five statements, identify the man in each position.

1. Mike and Dale were both at the ball park when the rookie pitcher played his first game.

2. Both Paul and the athletic director had played on the same team in high school with the goalie.

3. The athletic director, who scouted Charlie, is planning to watch Mike during his next game.

4. Mike doesn't know Dale.

5. One of these men is a quarterback.

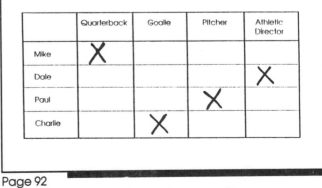

|  | Quarterback | Goalie | Pitcher | Athletic Director |
|---|---|---|---|---|
| Mike | X |  |  |  |
| Dale |  |  |  | X |
| Paul |  |  | X |  |
| Charlie |  | X |  |  |

**Page 92**

## Ordered Pairs and Graphing

Keep in mind...
Challenges make you discover things about yourself
that you never really knew.

– Cicely Tyson

### Plotting Points

Connect each of the following ordered points.

$(x, y) = (0, -1)$
— vertical move ⟹ down one
— horizontal move ⟹ no move

"Ancient History"

Start at (0, -1)

| | |
|---|---|
| (1, 1) | (0, 3) |
| (1, -3) | (-1, 4) |
| (3, -3) | (-2, 3) |
| (3, -1) | (-3, 4) |
| (5, 0) | (-4, 3) |
| (8, 0) | (-5, 0) |
| (7, 1) | (-8, 2) |
| (9, 0) | (-5, 0) |
| (8, 2) | (-3, -1) |
| (5, 1) | (-3, 3) |
| (4, 3) | (-1, -3) |
| (3, 4) | (-1, 4) |
| (2, 3) | (0, -1) |
| (1, 4) | End |

Page 93

## Ordered Pairs and Graphing

### Coordinates and Graphing

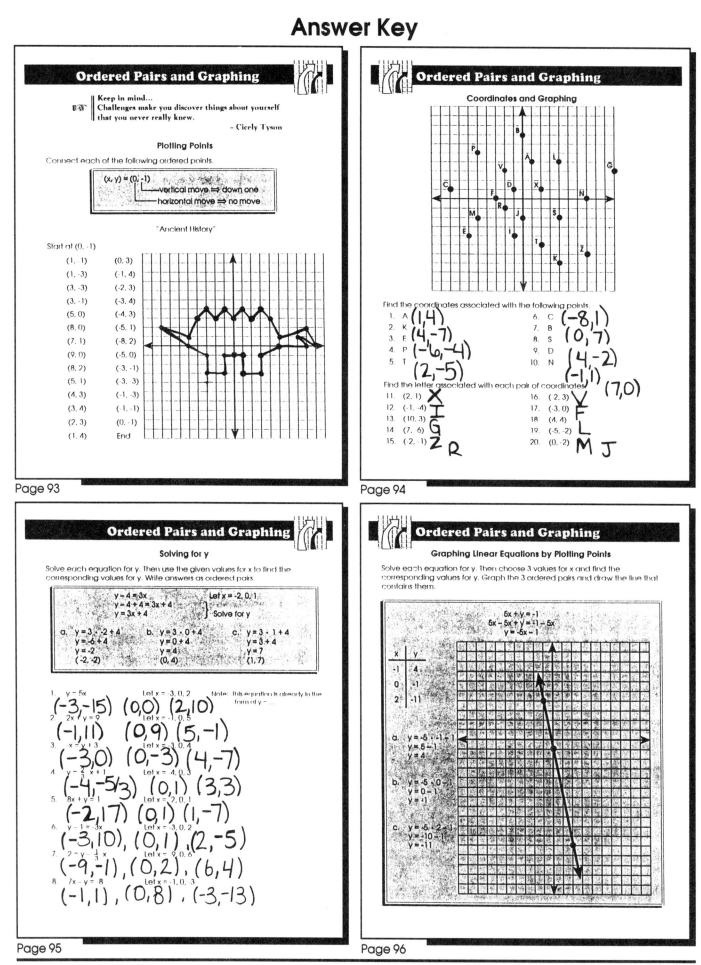

Find the coordinates associated with the following points.

1. A  (1, 4)
2. K  (4, -7)
3. E  (-6, -4)
4. P  (2, -5)
5. T

6. C  (-8, 1)
7. B  (0, 7)
8. S  (4, -2)
9. D  (-1, 1)
10. N  (7, 0)

Find the letter associated with each pair of coordinates.

11. (2, 1)  X
12. (-1, -4)  H
13. (10, 3)  G
14. (7, 6)  Z
15. (-2, -1)  R

16. (2, 3)  V
17. (-3, 0)  F
18. (4, 4)  L
19. (-5, -2)  M
20. (0, -2)  J

Page 94

## Ordered Pairs and Graphing

### Solving for y

Solve each equation for y. Then use the given values for x to find the corresponding values for y. Write answers as ordered pairs.

$y - 4 = 3x$
$y - 4 + 4 = 3x + 4$  Let x = -2, 0, 1.
$y = 3x + 4$  Solve for y

a. $y = 3 \cdot -2 + 4$   b. $y = 3 \cdot 0 + 4$   c. $y = 3 \cdot 1 + 4$
$y = -6 + 4$      $y = 0 + 4$      $y = 3 + 4$
$y = -2$        $y = 4$        $y = 7$
$(-2, -2)$       $(0, 4)$       $(1, 7)$

1. $y = 5x$  Let x = -3, 0, 2.  Note: This equation is already in the form of y = ...
(-3, -15) (0, 0) (2, 10)

2. $2x + y = 9$  Let x = -1, 0, 5.
(-1, 11) (0, 9) (5, -1)

3. $-x + y = 3$  Let x = -3, 0, 4.
(-3, 0) (0, -3) (4, -7)

4. $y = \frac{2}{3}x + 1$  Let x = -4, 0, 3.
(-4, -5/3) (0, 1) (3, 3)

5. $8x + y = 1$  Let x = -2, 0, 1.
(-2, 17) (0, 1) (1, -7)

6. $y - 1 = -3x$  Let x = -3, 0, 2.
(-3, 10), (0, 1), (2, -5)

7. $2 - y = \frac{1}{3}x$  Let x = -9, 0, 6.
(-9, -1), (0, 2), (6, 4)

8. $7x - y = 8$  Let x = -1, 0, 3.
(-1, 1), (0, 8), (-3, -13)

Page 95

## Ordered Pairs and Graphing

### Graphing Linear Equations by Plotting Points

Solve each equation for y. Then choose 3 values for x and find the corresponding values for y. Graph the 3 ordered pairs and draw the line that contains them.

$5x + y = -1$
$5x - 5x + y = -1 - 5x$
$y = -5x - 1$

| x | y |
|---|---|
| -1 | 4 |
| 0 | -1 |
| 2 | -11 |

a. $y = -5 \cdot -1 - 1$
$y = 5 - 1$
$y = 4$

b. $y = -5 \cdot 0 - 1$
$y = 0 - 1$
$y = -1$

c. $y = -5 \cdot 2 - 1$
$y = -10 - 1$
$y = -11$

Page 96

# Answer Key

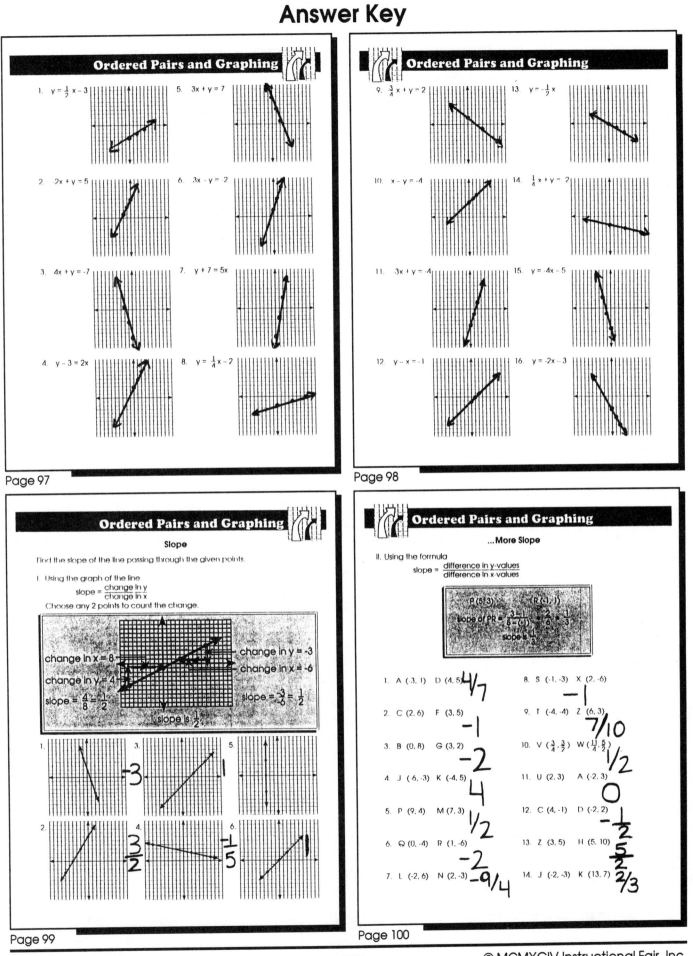

## Ordered Pairs and Graphing

1. $y = \frac{1}{2}x - 3$
5. $3x + y = 7$
2. $-2x + y = 5$
6. $3x - y = 2$
3. $4x + y = -7$
7. $y + 7 = 5x$
4. $y - 3 = 2x$
8. $y = \frac{1}{4}x - 2$

Page 97

## Ordered Pairs and Graphing

9. $\frac{3}{4}x + y = 2$
13. $y = -\frac{1}{2}x$
10. $x - y = -4$
14. $\frac{1}{4}x + y = 2$
11. $-3x + y = -4$
15. $y = -4x - 5$
12. $y - x = -1$
16. $y = -2x - 3$

Page 98

## Ordered Pairs and Graphing
### Slope

Find the slope of the line passing through the given points.

I. Using the graph of the line
$$\text{slope} = \frac{\text{change in } y}{\text{change in } x}$$
Choose any 2 points to count the change.

change in $x = 8$    change in $y = -3$

change in $y = 4$    change in $x = -6$

$\text{slope} = \frac{4}{8} = \frac{1}{2}$    $\text{slope} = \frac{-3}{-6} = \frac{1}{2}$

slope is $\frac{1}{2}$

1.
2.
3. $-3$
4. $\frac{3}{2}$
5. $1$
6. $-\frac{1}{5}$

Page 99

## Ordered Pairs and Graphing
### ...More Slope

II. Using the formula
$$\text{slope} = \frac{\text{difference in } y\text{-values}}{\text{difference in } x\text{-values}}$$

$P(5,3)$    $R(-1,1)$

$\text{slope of } PR = \frac{3-1}{5-(-1)} = \frac{2}{6} = \frac{1}{3}$

slope is $\frac{1}{3}$

1. A $(-3, 1)$   D $(4, 5)$   $4/7$
2. C $(2, 6)$   F $(3, 5)$   $-1$
3. B $(0, 8)$   G $(3, 2)$   $-2$
4. J $(6, -3)$   K $(-4, 5)$   $4$
5. P $(9, 4)$   M $(7, 3)$   $1/2$
6. Q $(0, -4)$   R $(1, -6)$   $-2$
7. L $(-2, 6)$   N $(2, -3)$   $-9/4$

8. S $(-1, -3)$   X $(2, -6)$   $-1$
9. T $(-4, -4)$   Z $(6, 3)$   $7/10$
10. V $(\frac{3}{4}, \frac{3}{2})$   W $(1\frac{1}{4}, \frac{5}{2})$   $1/2$
11. U $(2, 3)$   A $(-2, 3)$   $0$
12. C $(4, -1)$   D $(-2, 2)$   $-\frac{1}{2}$
13. Z $(3, 5)$   H $(5, 10)$   $\frac{5}{2}$
14. J $(-2, -3)$   K $(13, 7)$   $2/3$

Page 100

# Answer Key

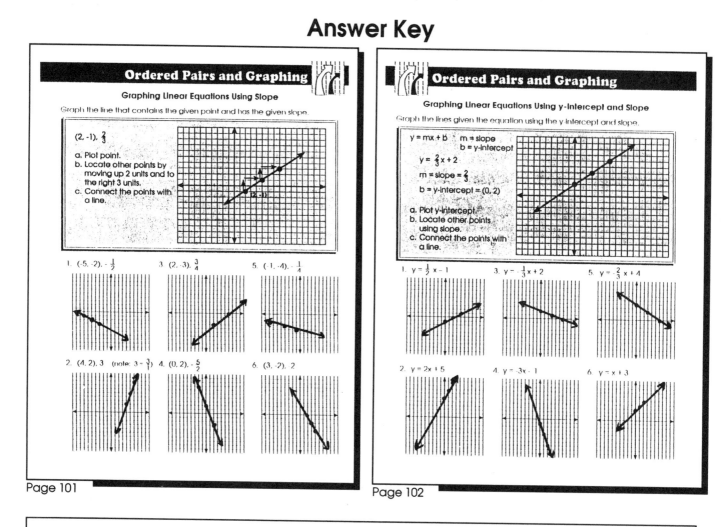

## About the Book . . .

This book has been designed to provide your student with practice in the necessary skill areas involved in mastering Pre-Algebra concepts. A review of basic skills is presented in the first part of the book and more specific Algebra topics are introduced on a gradual basis throughout the book. Each skill addressed is identified on all the activity pages and examples of solution methods are included for every skill.

## About the Author . . .

Mary Lee Vivian has helped many secondary students master a variety of mathematical skills during her 10 years of teaching in the Parkway School District in St. Louis, Missouri. She holds a Bachelor of Arts Degree in Mathematics from Central Methodist College and a Masters Degree in Business Administration from the University of Missouri – St. Louis. Currently taking time off to be at home with her two children, Mary Lee tutors students in secondary math.

## Credits . . .

*Author:* Mary Lee Vivian
*Artist/Production:* Emily Georg-Smith
*Project Director:* Mina McMullin
*Editors:* George Van Zwalenberg, Suzanne Hentz
*Cover Design:* Annette Hollister-Papp